eclipse

Inspire your Geographers of the future

Ian Mack

www.heinemann.co.uk
✓ Free online support
✓ Useful weblinks
✓ 24 hour online ordering

01865 888058

Heinemann Educational Publishers
Halley Court, Jordan Hill, Oxford, OX2 8EJ
Part of Harcourt Education
Heinemann is the registered trademark of
Harcourt Education Limited

© Harcourt Education, 2006

First published 2006

09 08 07 06
10 9 8 7 6 5 4 3 2 1

10-digit ISBN: 0 4353 4031 X
13-digit ISBN: 987 0 435 340315

British Library Cataloguing in Publication Data is
available from the British Library on request

Copyright notice.
All rights reserved. No part of this publication may be
reproduced in any form or by any means (including
photocopying or storing it in any medium by electronic
means and whether or not transiently or incidentally to
some other use of this publication) without the prior
written permission of the copyright owner, except in
accordance with the provisions of the Copyright, Designs
and Patents Act 1988 or under the terms of a licence
issued by the Copyright Licensing Agency Ltd, 90
Tottenham Court Road, London W1T 4LP. Applications
for the copyright owner's written permission to reproduce
any part of this publication should be addressed to the
publisher.

Designed by Wooden Ark Studio
Produced by Bridge Creative Services Ltd, Bicester, Oxon

Printed and bound at Scotprint, East Lothian

Index compiled by Derek Copson

Original illustrations © Harcourt Education Limited, 2006

Illustrated by Roger Farrington and Gary Wing

Photograph acknowledgements
The authors and publisher would like to thank the
following for permission to reproduce photographs:
Photo 1 (page 1) ; photo 2 (page 2) Arco Images/Alamy;
photo 3 and 4 (page 3) credit?; photo 7 (page 6) Rick
Colls/Rex Features; photo 8 (page 11) Simmons Aerofilms
Ltd/Alamy; photo 9 (page 11) Corbis UK Ltd; photo 10
(page 12) PCL/Alamy; photo 11 (page 13) Konrad
Zelazowski/Alamy; photo 11A (page 15) Reuters/Corbis UK
Ltd. photo 12 (page 17) Konrad Zelazowski/Alamy; photo
14 (page 19) Paul A. Souders/Corbis UK Ltd.; photo 15
(page 20) oote boe/Alamy; photo 16 (page 20) Ronald W.
Weir/Zefa/Corbis UK Ltd; photo 17 (page 21) Mary Evans
Picture Library; photo 18 (page 27) Colin Shepherd/Rex
Features; photo 19 (page 29) Image courtesy Jesse Allen,
based on data from the MODIS Rapid Response Team at
NASA GSFC/NASA; photo 20 (page 30) Photofusion
Picture Library/Alamy; photo 21 (page 33) Yann Arthus-
Bertrand/Corbis UK Ltd. photo 22 (page 34) Digital
Nation/Photofusion Picture Library; photo 24 (page 36)
Florence Boos; photo 25 (page 37) Florence Boos; photo
26 (page 37) Simmons Aerofilms Ltd/Alamy; photo 27
(page 39) Colin Skears/Fotolibra; photo 28 (page 41) Mike
Goldwater/Alamy; photo 29 (page 41) Ashley
Cooper/Corbis UK Ltd.; photo 32 (page 45) Graham
Dance/Fotolibra; photo 33 (page 47) London Aerial Photo
Library/Corbis UK Ltd; photo 34 (page 47) Bob
Watkins/Photofusion Picture Library; photo 35 (page 53)
Steven May/Alamy; photo 36 (page 54) Jim
Craigmyle/Corbis UK Ltd; photo 36A (page49) Carsten
Rehder/Dpa/Corbis UK Ltd.photo 37 (page 57)
Photofusion Picture Library; photo 38 (page 58) Peter
Macdiarmid/Getty Images; photo 39 (page 60) Kevin
Foy/Alamy; photo 40 (page 61) Janine Wiedel
Photolibrary/Alamy; photo 41 (page 63) AP Photo/Richard
Vogel/Empics; photo 42 (page 64) Getty Images; photo
42A (67) Digital Art/Corbis UK Ltd; photo 43 (page 70)
Alex Segre/Alamy; photo 44 (page 72) NASA Marshall
Space Flight Center (NASA-MSFC)/NASA; photo 45 (page
73) Mark M. Lawrence/Corbis UK Ltd; photo 46 (page 74)
AsiaSat; photo 47 (page 76) Getty Images/PhotoDisc
/60205/; photo 48 (page /8) Created by the National
Center for Supercomputing Applications (NCSA) at the
University of Illinois at Urbana-Champaign / Copyright
1994 The Board of Trustees of the University of
Illinois/University of Illinois at Urbana Champaign NCSA;
photo 49 (page 79) Martin Dodge, University of
Manchester, www.cybergeography.org; photo 50 (page 80)
University of California San Diego; photo 51 (page 81)
Interoute Communications Limited; photo 51A (page 87)
Tesco Stores Limited ; photo 52 (page 88) Photofusion
Picture Library/Alamy; photo 53 (90) Photofusion Picture
Library; photo 54 (page 91) Don Gray/Photofusion Picture
Library; photo 55 (page 92) Janine Wiedel
Photolibrary/Alamy; photo 56 (page 94) Paul
Yeung/Reuters/Corbis UK Ltd; photo 57 (page 95) contact
Photographers Direct/Robert Crook; photo 58 (page 97)
Marianna Day Massey/Zuma/Corbis UK Ltd; photo 59
(page 98) The Fairtrade Foundation

Cover photograph by Photolibrary/Workbook Inc.

Picture research by Zooid Pictures Ltd.

The publisher would like to thank the following for
permission to reproduce copyright material:

Figure 2 on page 4 is reproduced by permission of
Ordnance Survey on behalf of HMSO.
© Crown copyright 2006. All rights reserved. Ordnance
Licence Number 100000230
The extract on page 59 is reproduced with permission of
Guardian Newspapers Limited.

The publishers have made every effort to trace copyright
holders. However, if any material has been incorrectly
acknowledged, we would be pleased to correct this at the
earliest opportunity.

CONTENTS

Chapter 1 Place — 1
- **1.1** What is place? — 2
- **1.2** My place — 4
- **1.3** Same place, different place? — 6
- **1.4** A sense of place — 8
- **1.5** Linking places: interdependence — 9
- **1.6** Changing place — 10
- **1.7** Representing place — 11
- **1.8** Forbidden place; emotional place — 12

Chapter 2 Climate — 15
- **2.1** What is climate? An introduction — 16
- **2.2** Has our climate changed? — 18
- **2.3** The evidence for climate change — 20
- **2.4** Explaining climate change 1: natural causes — 22
- **2.5** Explaining climate change 2: human causes — 24
- **2.6** Consequences of climate change — 26
- **2.7** The climate change debate — 28
- **2.8** Is there a solution to climate change? — 29

Chapter 3 Planning in Britain — 33
- **3.1** The built environment — 34
- **3.2** Victorian London — 35
- **3.3** The garden city — 36
- **3.4** The New Towns — 38
- **3.5** Planning at the national level — 40
- **3.6** Planning at the regional level — 42
- **3.7** Planning at the local level — 44
- **3.8** The Coin Street community — 46

Chapter 4 Globalisation — 49
- **4.1** What is globalisation? — 50
- **4.2** A shrinking world 1: transport — 52
- **4.3** A shrinking world 2: communications — 54
- **4.4** Joining the world together — 56
- **4.5** Changing places — 58
- **4.6** Global power: countries or companies? — 60
- **4.7** Nike, a global company — 62
- **4.8** Global products, global culture — 64

Chapter 5 Cybergeography — 67
- **5.1** What is cybergeography? — 68
- **5.2** What is cyberspace? — 70
- **5.3** A space of flows — 73
- **5.4** Changing the real world — 74
- **5.5** Singapore, a wired city — 76
- **5.6** Mapping cyberspace — 78
- **5.7** Holes in cyberspace — 82
- **5.8** The death of real places — 84

Chapter 6 Geographies of consumption — 87
- **6.1** People as consumers — 88
- **6.2** Right or responsibility? — 89
- **6.3** Consumption in the landscape — 90
- **6.4** The prouction-consumption chain — 93
- **6.5** The effect of our decisions — 94
- **6.6** Who decides? — 96
- **6.7** The coolhunters — 97
- **6.8** Fair trade — 98

Glossary — 101
Index — 103

INTRODUCTION

This geography textbook is, in several ways, unlike any other. It aims to re-link school geography with the geographies which have been taught in universities since the National Curriculum was written. It seems to me that school geography and university geography have become entirely different subjects; and this book goes some way to closing the divide between them.

Each chapter is designed to be used independently, and could form the basis of a challenging and interesting unit of work. There is no need to start at the beginning of the book, nor to worry about deviating from the National Curriculum: the chapters have creative links to the KS3 curriculum.

This book offers a discussion of some fascinating aspects of contemporary geography. By encouraging creative and stimulating teaching, it aims to facilitate students' learning and fire up their geographical imaginations.

Ian Mack
University of Central England

Chapter 1

Place

1.1 What is place?
1.2 My place
1.3 Same place, different place?
1.4 A sense of place
1.5 Linking places: interdependence
1.6 Changing place
1.7 Representing place
1.8 Forbidden place; emotional place

1.1 What is place?

If you were asked to name a place you knew, you would probably mention a particular location. For example, if you lived in the West Midlands, you might say that you knew Birmingham – perhaps because it is the largest city in the West Midlands. So, the word 'place' often means a particular location.

In geography, the word 'place' also has other meanings. It is used to describe:

- locations with which we have a particular link, such as the area where you were born, or where you have relatives
- locations of which we have experience, such as the place in which you live, or somewhere you visit regularly, or a place where something memorable happened.

Place and space

Geographers mean different things when they use the terms 'place' and 'space'. Try thinking of space as all the locations on the earth – most of us will have no connection with the vast majority of these locations and are unlikely to have any knowledge of them. Place, however, refers to the locations we know ourselves – in other words, places that mean something to us or those with which we have a connection.

The idea of place is central to geography – which is why it comes first in this book – because geography is the study of the relationship between people and places.

Places, then, are an important part of our everyday lives and experience. One geographer has suggested that our lives take place within 'activity spaces' – these are a network of all the places we visit. Figure 1 gives an example.

● **Figure 1** St Peter Port: Place for some people, space for others

● **Figure 2** A geography teacher's activity spaces

Action Point

It's time now to think of the places in your own life. First, write a list of all the places you have visited in the past seven days – and the reasons you went to them.

Next, using an atlas or globe, write a list of five locations in the world that you have never been to, or have no connection with.

Which of your lists refers to place, and which to space? Can you see any patterns in the locations you have chosen?

Action Point

Draw a diagram of your own 'activity spaces'. Include all the places you visit regularly and also those you visit only occasionally. Compare your diagram with someone else's. Identify how your 'activity spaces' differ, and try to work out why.

What makes a place distinctive?

Geographers often refer to a particular location as having a 'sense of place'. What this means is that the place has distinctive characteristics or features that make it unique. You might think of every place as having its own identity, in the same way as every person has their own identity (such as their appearance, or what they wear).

But what is it about a place that makes it distinctive, and gives it a 'sense of place'? Think about the following factors:

- The shape of the land. Is it flat? Is it hilly?
- The built environment. What are the buildings like? Is it more rural than urban?
- The people. What are the people like? Is there a local accent? What are their daily routines?
- The climate. What is the annual rainfall? What is the annual range of temperature?
- Your own experience of the place. Do you associate the place with a particular visit or event? Did something memorable happen there? What is your opinion of the place?

Of course, these are only some of the factors that make every place unique. If you removed or changed some of those factors, the 'sense of place' would alter in some way. For example, if all Londoners spoke with a Geordie accent, or Buckingham Palace was relocated to Manchester, the locations would have an entirely different sense of place. The particular factors that made them unique would change. For example, look at these aerial photographs of London. In the first photograph, you can see the Houses of Parliament. In the second photograph, what impact does the 'disappearance' of these buildings have on London's 'sense of place'?

> **Think Point**
>
> What makes the area where you live distinctive? Draw a spider diagram to identify the features that make it unique. Try to add as much detail as you can. Then try to imagine the place without one of those characteristics. How would it change?

● **Figure 3** The Houses of Parliament in London

● **Figure 4** What happens to London's sense of place when the Houses of Parliament 'disappear' from the scene?

1.2 My place

If someone asked you where you came from, you would probably tell them the name of the place you think of as home. If you live in a town or a city, you might name a particular district or **suburb**; if you live in a rural area, you might name the nearest village. Wherever you live, it is likely that you will have a place you call home – the place you identify with the most strongly – and this is what geographers mean by 'my place'.

Studying 'my place'

Of course, this book cannot tell you about the geography of your place, but it can give you some ideas to help you investigate it yourself. Your local area is a useful place to study in detail. If you work towards understanding your place well, the knowledge and skills you gain in doing so will help you to understand other places too – and that will make you a better geographer!

> **Think Point**
>
> Identify the area you would call your place. Think about the reasons why you have chosen that particular place, perhaps in preference to another place.

> **Action Point**
>
> Geographers are well known for being inquisitive and are good investigators. Now it's time to research your place. The table opposite includes some questions that you could ask about your place, and some suggestions for discovering the answers.

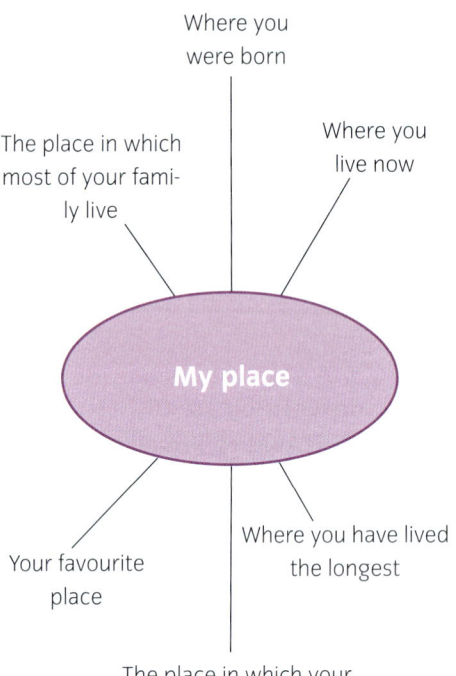

Figure 1 Where is my place?

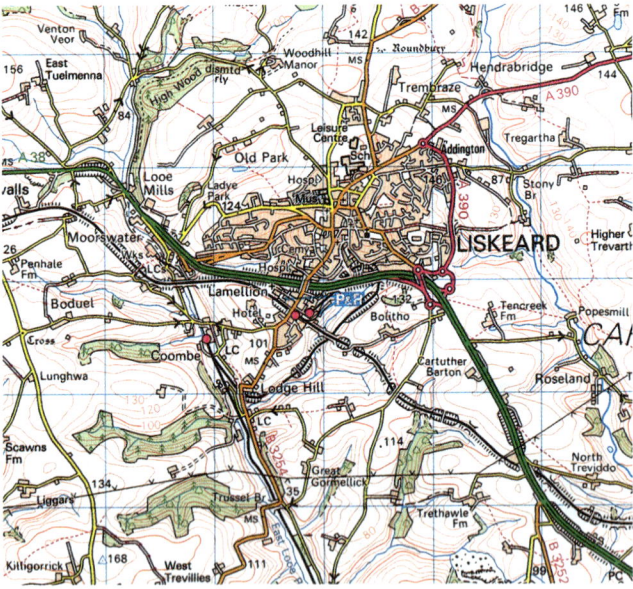

Figure 2 Researching 'my place' – maps at different scales

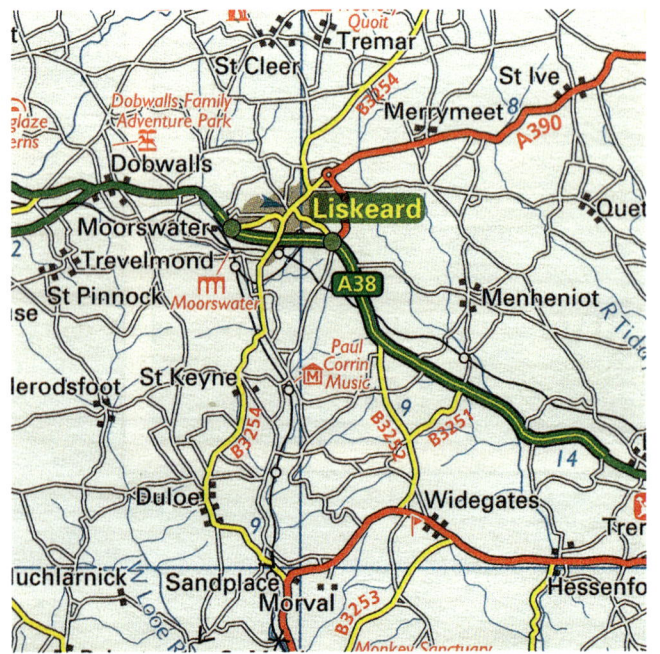

Presenting 'my place'

Having researched your place carefully, you will now need to think about how to present your findings. Good presentation skills are valued in geography, because they help us to communicate our ideas clearly.

Geographical questions about 'my place'	Ways to find the answer	Ideas you could use
Where is my place in relation to other places?	Look at local and national maps.	Try to use maps at a range of scales. You could use a mapping website.
What is it like here?	Find some modern photographs, or take your own. Describe what your place is like. Think carefully about its sense of place.	Think about the five senses (touch, taste, sight, sound and smell). Is there more to your place than its appearance?
How does it link to other places?	Investigate transport networks – road, rail and bus. Look at air or sea transport if appropriate. Why do people travel to and from your place? Which goods and services travel to and from your place?	Try showing the links on a map. Is it possible to identify different types of links, such as flows of goods, people or information?
What is my opinion of my place?	What do I like about my place? What do I like least?	Do your friends think similarly or differently? What about other people that you know?
What is the identity of my place?	How is your place portrayed in the media, such as the Internet, travel brochures and newspapers? How does your place advertise itself? Does your place have a distinctive history? Is it famous for something in particular? Does your place feature in the news, for example on television or in the newspapers?	Does your place have a website? How does it portray your place? Why is your place shown in a particular way?
What are the big geographical issues here?	There could be many issues! For example: planning applications for roads, supermarkets, housing, etc., or issues to do with jobs, the environment, or social issues such as crime or homelessness. To find out about these, look in your local newspapers; listen to your local radio station or watch news reports on regional television.	Ask around. Use as many sources of information as you can. Websites may be helpful – use a search engine carefully by typing in the name of your place and then words like 'employment' or 'news'. The BBC News website may be a useful resource.

You could, of course, write up the results of your investigation in an exercise book, but you could also:

- create a colourful and informative classroom display
- prepare a PowerPoint presentation using words, images (and maybe even sounds)
- make a brochure using desk top publishing software, or use a digital camera or camcorder to illustrate an article about your place.

You should assume that your audience are geographers from another part of the UK. Try to make it clear exactly what your place is like, and how you feel about it. Before you finish your work, check carefully that it is well written, illustrated using pictures or diagrams, and is professionally presented.

Learning Point

Before we continue, let's check that you understand:

- what geographers mean by 'place'
- the difference between 'place' and 'space'
- which places link to your every-day life ('activity spaces')
- what geographers mean by a 'sense of place'
- the geographical features of 'your place'
- why your place is distinctive, and has its own 'sense of place'.

1.3 Same place, different place?

Think of a place you know well – perhaps a local town or city, or the nearest village. Now think of the people in that place. Do you think they all feel the same way about the place you have in mind? Is it likely that people think identically about it, or differently?

Think Point

Why may some people think similarly, and others differently, about the same place?

Action Point

Let's assume that the area around your school is 'your place'. Write down ten adjectives you might use to describe 'your place'. Now compare your answers with others in your class. What are the similarities and the differences? Can you think of reasons to explain the differences?

Geographers suggest that different people may think about the same place in entirely different ways. Our minds work independently; we may all have had contrasting experiences in the same place. This might be because people come from different backgrounds, because they have differing values and opinions, or simply because we are all individuals. Here's an example based around Birmingham city centre.

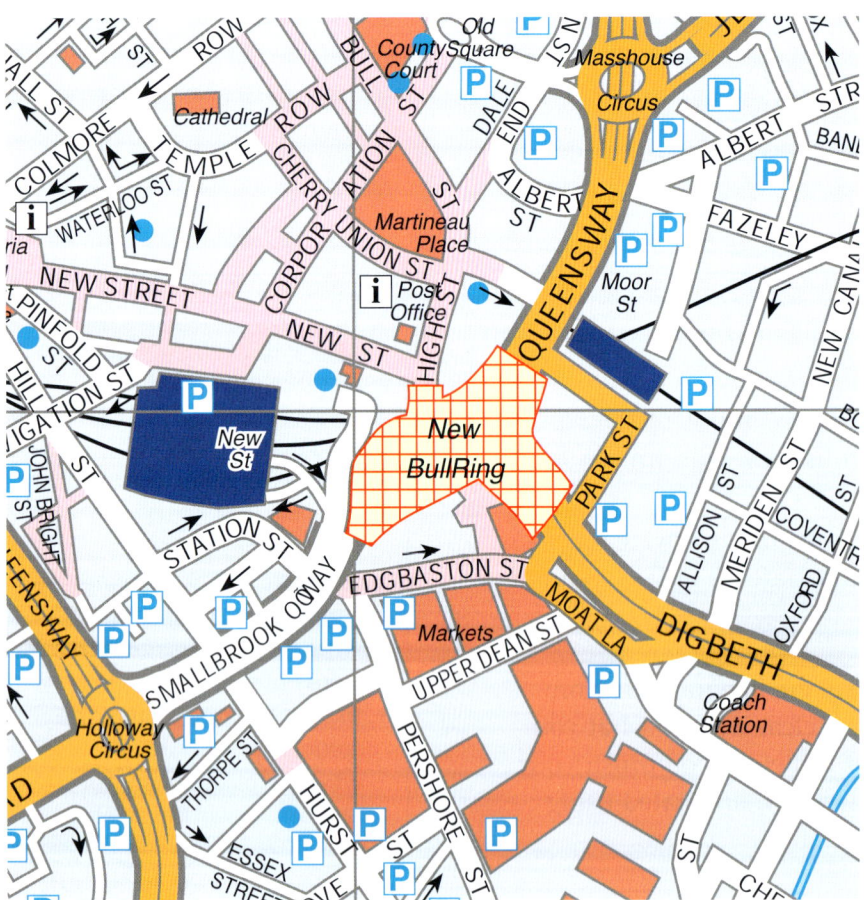

● **Figure 1** A map of central Birmingham

● **Figure 2** Central Birmingham

'I like Birmingham city centre. I have an interesting and well-paid job based in the heart of the city. After work, I can relax without travelling very far. There are wine bars, restaurants and cafés in some rather upmarket locations – my favourites are by the canal side. I have my own parking space at the office, but I don't really use it because I live in The Mailbox – an exclusive, city centre housing development in the former post office.'

Rachel, lawyer, 38

'I don't come to Birmingham very often. When I do, it's usually in the evening – the nightlife along Broad Street is fantastic. I don't see much of central Birmingham otherwise, apart from the occasional Saturday when my parents visit – they like to visit the city centre shops. I don't shop in the city centre usually. I normally shop in the local, suburban supermarket. Sometimes I treat myself to a trip to the city centre Selfridges, which is in the Bullring, usually after I've been paid for my part-time bar job.'

Emma, student, 21

'I come to Birmingham city centre because it's warmer than the rest of the city. The heat from the city centre shops and offices helps – I have to sleep in doorways at night. There are plenty of passers-by in the daytime; many of them clearly have money, but I don't see much of it. I feel as if I'm invisible sometimes. There's no chance of my getting a job – I can't get the skills or the home I need. Birmingham city centre means poverty to me.'

Darren, homeless, 27

Mustafa, immigrant, 36

'I meet other people who have come here from Turkey near the fountains on New Street. It's the only place I can meet people who speak the same language as me. Birmingham doesn't feel like home to me – it just feels alien. I'm only here because I needed to leave Turkey. This isn't my home and I don't feel attached to Birmingham. I do some part-time work in a warehouse just outside the city centre. The pay is low, but the council put me up in a bed and breakfast. I don't know how long that will last though.'

Action Point

Now, think again about 'your place'. First, make a list of the different 'types' of people you see there, e.g. teenagers, office workers, visitors. Try to work out how individuals from those different groups of people might feel about 'your place'. Think about the reasons they might be there, and the experience they have of the place. Why might they think differently?

1.4 A sense of place

At the beginning of the chapter we looked at the things that make a place distinctive. Now, we need to ask: How do we know that one place is different from another? Why do we feel differently about some places than others?

The answer may be that everywhere has a certain 'sense of place' – a mix of qualities that makes a place unique.

Information about the world comes to us through the five senses: sight, sound, touch, smell and taste. These are the only ways in which information reaches us and, once it has arrived, our brain tries to make sense of it.

Places stimulate all our senses at once. If we were standing in Trafalgar Square in the middle of London, for example, we would be able to see some well-known landmarks, to hear the traffic and people around us, perhaps to touch Nelson's Column, to smell the traffic fumes. Even the air might have a distinctive 'London' taste. All these qualities give Trafalgar Square a particular sense of place – they make it unique.

● **Figure 1** A sense of place

Think Point

Think about a place you know well. Would it have the same sense of place at different times of day? How and why would it differ?

Action Point

Choose a place you know well, such as the area around your school or home. What gives it a particular sense of place? How does the place trigger each of your five senses? Present your findings – you could write a poem or a haiku, or produce a PowerPoint presentation or a brochure.

As geographers, it is not enough just to describe a location's sense of place – we should also try to explain why it might be like that. The question we should ask is: which aspects or features of places trigger our own senses? As a starting point, think about buildings, the natural environment, the people, the sounds all around us, our previous experience of the place and its history. You may be able to think of many more reasons why a particular place means something to you.

1.5 Linking places: interdependence

We may not think about it very often, but places are linked to each other in a variety of ways. For example, there are roads and railways – and perhaps other transport links – that connect places to each other physically. There are many other links between places – a nearby town or city might provide jobs for the people in the place in which you live, or a school or business might serve people from a variety of different places. We call this linking of places interdependence.

Now think about the items we buy. Are they all made in the place we buy them from? More often than not, they are made or grown in another place, sometimes many thousands of miles away. When you next visit the local supermarket, look carefully at the products on the shelves to find out where they come from. You will probably find that you can take a virtual 'world tour'! It's amazing to think that a simple shopping trip can give us worldwide connections we never knew we had.

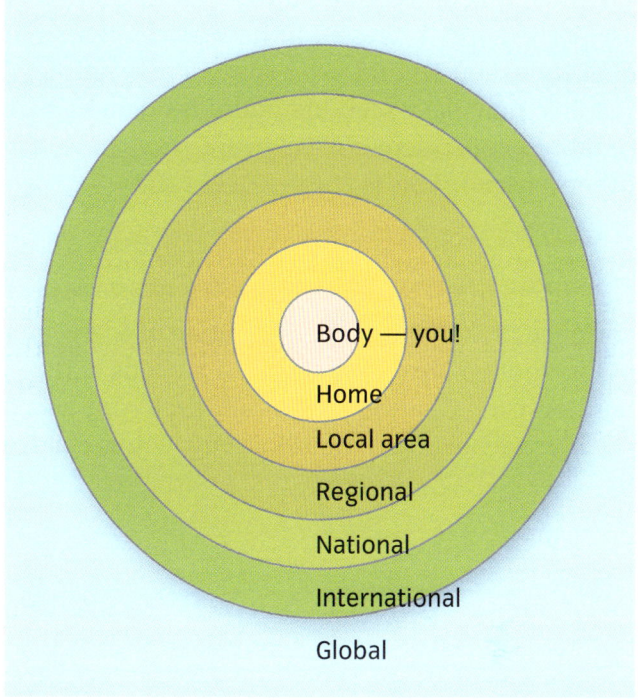

● **Figure 1** Geographers work with a whole range of different scales, starting with you.

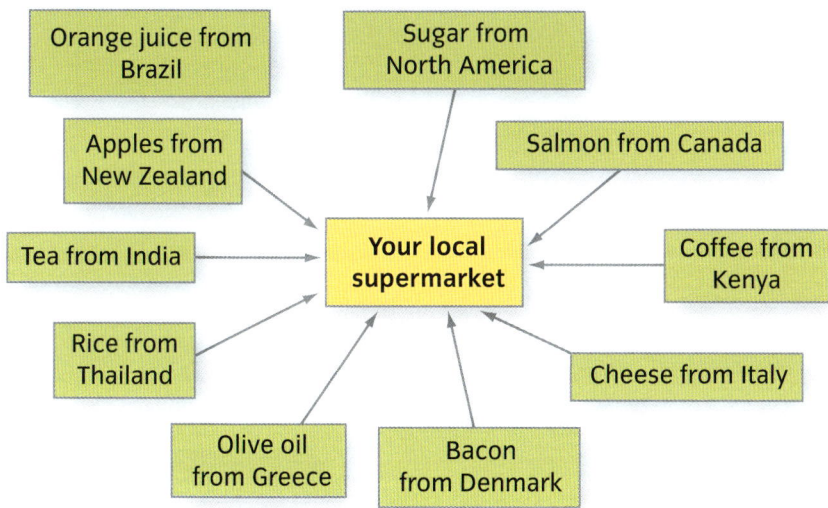

● **Figure 2** Take a world tour – via your supermarket

Geographers suggest that places depend on one another. You depend on food being produced elsewhere and arriving in time for you to eat it; and the food producers will rely on your money reaching them to pay for it. Similarly, our homes almost certainly depend on electricity produced elsewhere, and the cars many people use every day are manufactured in other parts of the world. Each of these examples reveals interdependence – the idea that places are not only connected, but that they rely on each other.

Action Point

How many places do you think you have links with? Think about what you do, what you eat, what you wear and where you go over a period of seven. Then write a list of ten links with other places. Now, share your results with others in the class. Plot the results on a local map.

Action Point

Think about a particular place you know well – such as the place you called 'my place' in section 1.2. How many connections can you think of between your place and other places? Now, using two blank maps, one of the UK and the other of the world, mark the places with which your place has links.

Chapter 1 Place

1.6 Changing place

We often take it for granted that places change. As geographers, we are particularly interested in how places change in two ways: first, over time, and second, over space. For example, the place in which you live may have seen old buildings demolished and new buildings constructed; some people may have left the area and others arrived. This is change over time.

In geography, though, we are interested in where changes occur as well as when. For example, think of a large city. At the same time, one area may be suffering from the closure of a large manufacturing plant, but in another area there may be a growing and successful high-tech business park. Changes are not limited to one area or district but occur unevenly across the whole city. This is change over space.

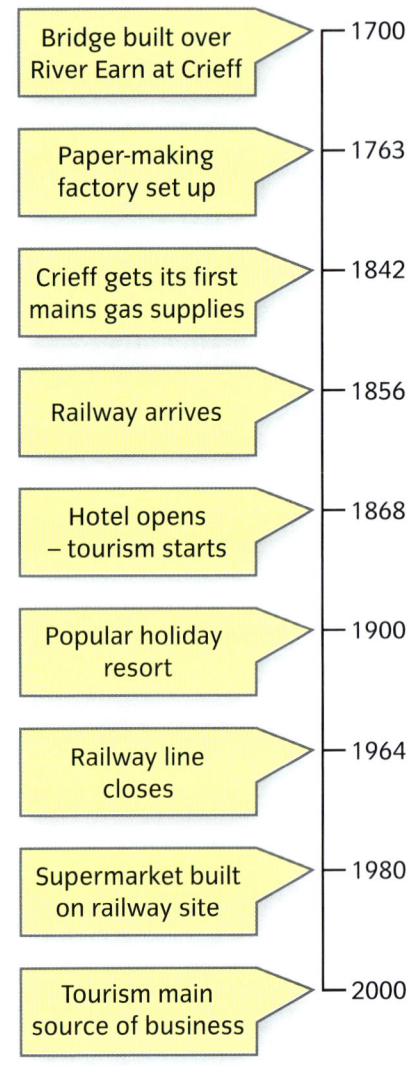

Figure 1 How the town of Crieff in Perthshire has changed over time
Source: the Strathearn website

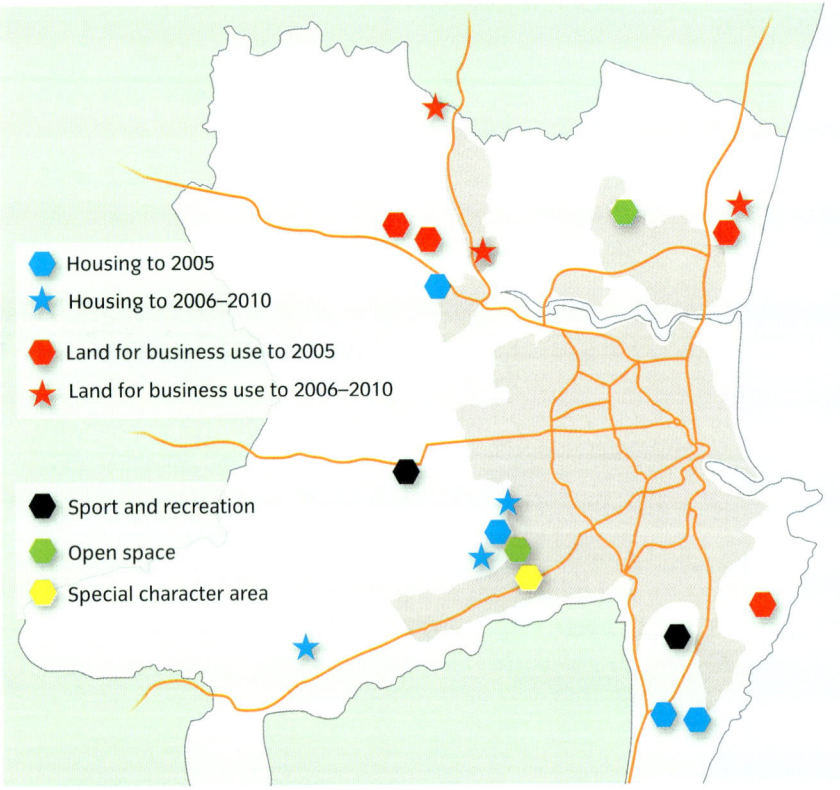

Figure 2 How Aberdeen is changing over space

Think Point

Can you identify any patterns in Figure 2?

Action Point

Now try to work out how your place has changed over time and space. First, find out how the place has changed over time. A good place to start might be your local library, the local newspaper or a website, or by asking local people you know. Once you have several examples of change, put them into chronological order using a timeline. Then plot the changes on a local map, making clear what took place and when it happened. You should now have a map showing local changes over time and space!

1.7 Representing place

We do not always need to visit a place to find out something about what it is like. We can get an image of a place through a variety of different media, such as photographs, paintings, writing, music, or a combination of different sources.

> **Think Point**
>
> Look at the pictures of Staffa. Do you think that paintings are an accurate way of portraying a place? Is a photograph a better, or simply a different, way? Is one method of representation more reliable than another?

● **Figure 1** Staffa, off the west coast of Scotland

As geographers, we need to understand that the way places are **represented** to us may sometimes be biased. For example, a holiday brochure is likely to make a place look attractive in order to sell holidays; a painting of a landscape is someone else's interpretation of what a place is like, in the painter's own style; and photographs can only show part of a place – the rest of the place may be entirely different.

> **Action Point**
>
> Read the passage about the Isle of Mull. Can you find any evidence of bias in the writing? Why was it written like this? What sort of publication might it have come from?

> 'The Isle of Mull is a place of tumbling burns, high peaks, dramatic views and a silent, lonely beauty. The multi-coloured buildings that line the waterfront of the island's principal town, Tobermory, will be familiar to many. Torosay Castle is a Scottish baronial gem, set among 12 acres of spectacular contrasting gardens. Nearby, Duart Castle, the 13th century home of the Chief of Clan MacLean, sits broodingly on its headland, seemingly unmoved by the stunning views across the Firth of Lorne to Ben Cruachan. Lying just off the Ross of Mull, the sacred isle of Iona is famous the world over for its peaceful Abbey, a place of calm and contemplation, the perfect antidote to the stress of modern life.'

Source: the Scotsman website

1.8 Forbidden place; emotional place

In the UK, people often say that we live in a 'free country'. From this, we might imagine that we may go to any place we wanted to visit, whether it is in the countryside or in a built-up area.

In practice, though, our movements are restricted. We do not have the freedom to go wherever we want. As geographers, we say that there are places from which we are **excluded**.

In your list you may well have included many examples of private property, where the owner has the right to exclude us, such as some government buildings, privately owned shopping centres (such as Bluewater in south-east England), royal palaces, or other people's houses and gardens.

Think Point

Make a list of some places that the general public may not enter. Start with your home area, then your local area, then regionally or nationally. Note down what prevents you from entering them.

Think Point

Think about your local area. From what proportion of it do you feel excluded? You could draw a map to help.

● **Figure 1** The public is generally excluded from royal palaces, although at Windsor Castle the public can pay to view certain areas

There are also places from which certain people may be excluded. By law, people under the age of 18 are not allowed in casinos, for example, and for health and safety reasons, the general public are excluded from building sites and schools.

Disabled people are also excluded from many places because they find access difficult or impossible. Despite a recent law to prevent this sort of discrimination, there are still places (such as some railway stations, shops and restaurants) from which disabled people are excluded.

Action Point

Next time you visit your nearest **urban settlement**, try to imagine getting around that place from the point of view of a wheelchair user. From which places might you be excluded? What measures could be taken to improve the situation?

Emotional places

Earlier in this chapter, we considered the idea of 'sense of place' – the unique nature of a place. Taking that idea a step further, a place might cause us to have certain feelings or emotions about the place. For example, in some places we may be anxious or frightened by it – perhaps in a dark churchyard, or an overcrowded area. Other places may make us feel happy and relaxed – perhaps when we are on holiday, or at home watching television with our family.

The key point is that places can suggest particular emotions in us – places can make us feel a certain way about them. As geographers, we use the terms topophilia (love of place) and topophobia (fear of place) to help us to understand the idea.

● **Figure 2** Some people find cemeteries emotional places

● **Figure 3** Topophilia and topophobia

Now that we know that can be excluded from certain places, we need also to consider that sometimes people exclude *themselves* from certain places. For example, we might try to avoid open spaces at night, or certain parts of cities that are known for a high crime rate. Although there is no physical barrier to our entering these places, fear (or sometimes simple common sense) causes us to exclude ourselves from them. Either way, our freedoms are restricted by our thoughts or emotions.

Action Point

Make a list of the emotions students might feel in various parts of your school. You might start your list with 'excitement' or 'nervousness'.

Using a base map of the school, try to plot the emotions you feel in various parts of the school. Try to include as many individual classrooms as you can, as well as corridors and other spaces – both inside and outside.

Colour code your map to make it as clear as possible to the reader. Give it the title 'An emotional geography of my school'. Compare your map with others in your class. Are they similar? If not, why might this be?

Learning Point

Before we continue, let's check that you understand:
- why people might have different opinions of the same place
- the variety of ways in which places depend on each other (interdependence)
- how places change over time *and* space
- why a 'sense of place' differs between places
- why places are represented in a variety of ways
- that people are excluded from many places
- that places can cause particular emotions within people.

Assessment

One idea that geographers are particularly interested in is that of 'alternative futures', whereby the future of a place is not fixed but can be shaped by people and natural processes. In this assessment, you will be asked to think about how your place may change in the future, and how its sense of place may change.

Choose a place you know well, such as the area you called 'my place'. For this area, carry out the following tasks:

1. Work out your personal vision of how you might like the area to change in the future, say over the next ten years. Remember that some changes take longer than others!
2. Present your vision based around a map, clearly identifying change over time (when might it happen?) and over space (where will it happen?).
3. Show how your area's sense of place might change as a result of your vision. You could think of your vision in terms of the five senses: sight, sound, touch, smell and taste. Under the heading of each sense, *describe* the changes and then *explain why* the change might take place.

As you work through each of the tasks, remember the importance of presentation – present what you have to say as clearly and as professionally as you can. Remember to use a variety of media – writing (perhaps in varied forms), photos, drawings and graphs where appropriate.

Chapter 2
Climate

- **2.1** What is climate? An introduction
- **2.2** Has our climate changed?
- **2.3** The evidence for climate change
- **2.4** Explaining climate change 1: natural causes
- **2.5** Explaining climate change 2: human causes
- **2.6** Consequences of climate change
- **2.7** The climate change debate
- **2.8** Is there a solution to climate change?

2.1 What is climate? An introduction

People in Britain often talk about the weather, even when it is rather ordinary, and when it is particularly hot, cold, wet or dry, people talk about the weather even more.

Think Point

What do you know about climate change or global warming? Draw a diagram to show your ideas. Keep this diagram safe. At the end of the chapter, you will be asked to look at it again to see whether your ideas have changed.

● **Figure 1** In Britain, we are always talking about the weather!

However, people often get confused about the difference between 'weather' and 'climate'. As geographers, we need to use the terms correctly.

Weather is what is happening now – the current state of the atmosphere. So, if you look out of the window, what you will see is weather. It includes temperature, precipitation (for example, rain, snow and hail), wind (speed and direction), cloud cover and sunshine.

Climate is the average of the weather conditions over a long period of time, generally 30 years. It is what the atmospheric conditions are *usually* like. Climatologists often concentrate on just two weather conditions when they look at climate: temperature and rainfall (precipitation).

One of the things someone planning a holiday abroad is likely to investigate before booking their tickets is the *climate* of the place, in order to find out what the weather is typically like at the time of year they want to go. Information about climate is usually shown in monthly blocks. If we look at the data in a graph, we can probably identify patterns within it. For example, in Britain, it generally gets gradually warmer in the spring, and gradually cooler in the autumn.

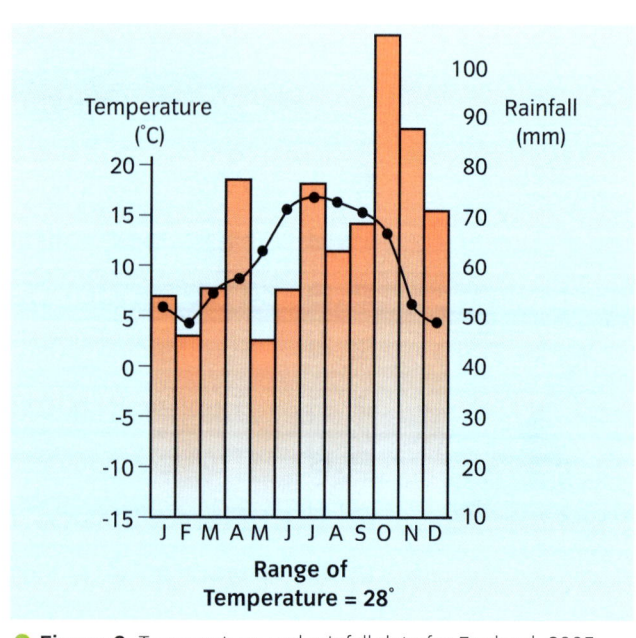

● **Figure 2** Temperature and rainfall data for England, 2005

16

Of course, once the person arrives at their holiday destination, they will experience what the *weather* is like during their stay. It may well be different from the climate they had expected – which would be the average of the weather conditions – but it will give them plenty to write about on their postcards home.

Action Point

Imagine you are writing an article for a travel website. Write a short paragraph explaining the difference between weather and climate.

This chapter, though, concentrates on climate – the long-term weather conditions. In particular, it looks at the issue of climate change. This is the idea that climate itself is altering, and that the earth as a whole is becoming warmer.

Climate change regularly makes the news. Some people are concerned that it will change the places we live in permanently; others argue that it is a natural process and that sometimes the earth heats up, and at other times it cools down. The aim of this chapter is to present you with some of the facts so that, having considered them, you will be able to decide for yourself.

● **Figure 3** British landscapes

Think Point

Look at the photograph above. How do you think the climate might have affected the coastline?
How do you think it might change in the future?

2.2 Has our climate changed?

Before we start to think about climate change, we need to consider some important facts. To begin with, let's look at how the earth's temperature has changed over time.

Scientists have been able to examine ice core samples taken from places like the Arctic to work out the earth's mean air temperature going back 850 million years! Figure 1 shows this information and also the current average air temperature.

> ### Think Point
> Using Figure 1, answer the following questions:
> a What is the mean air temperature in the 21st century so far?
> b When else has the earth's mean air temperature been 15°C or above?
> c What was the coldest mean temperature, and when did it occur?
> d What patterns can you identify?

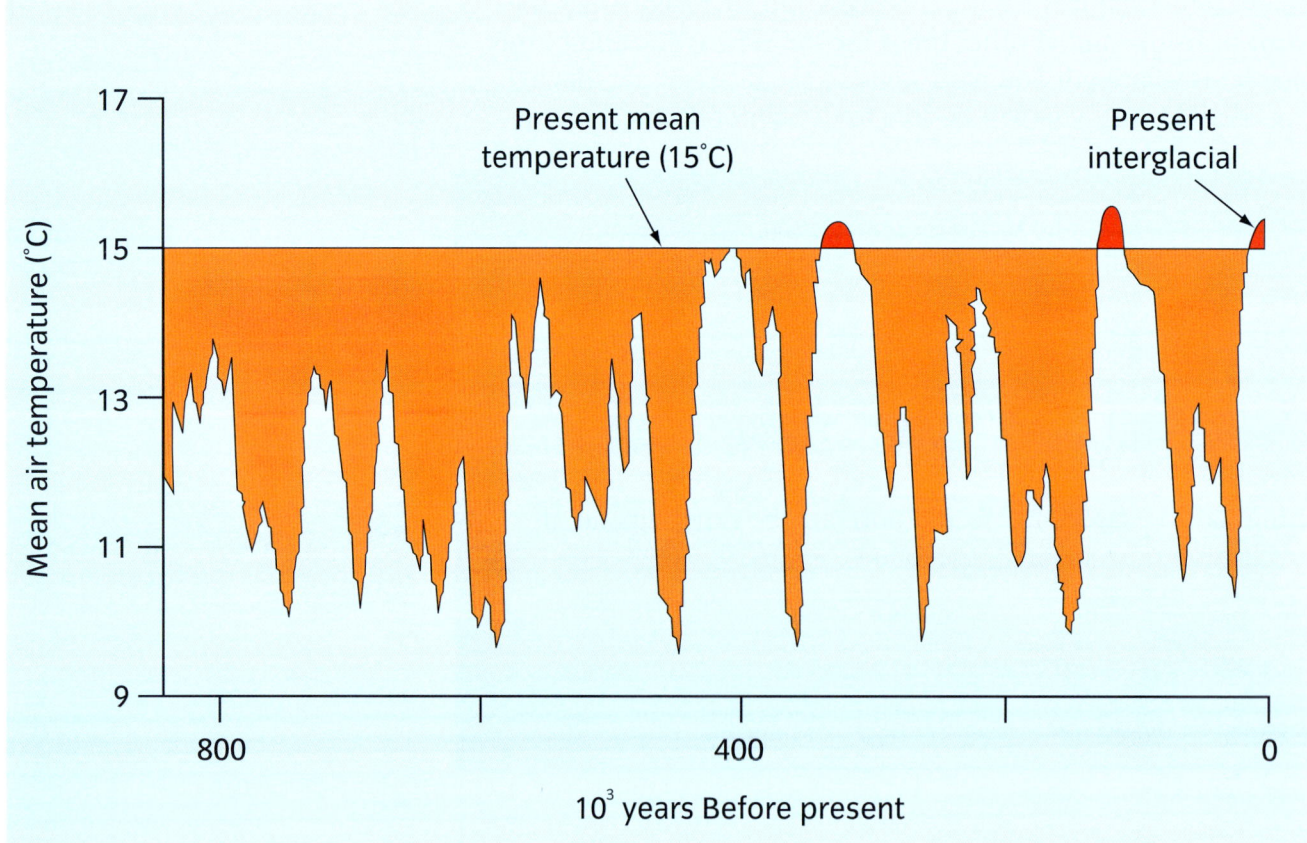

● **Figure 1** Climate graph from 850 million years ago to the present

If we look at Figure 1, we can see that the world's average temperature has always changed over time. However, if we look at data over a shorter period of time, the picture appears rather different. For example, Figure 2 shows data over the past 135 years – here the average temperature can be seen to rise.

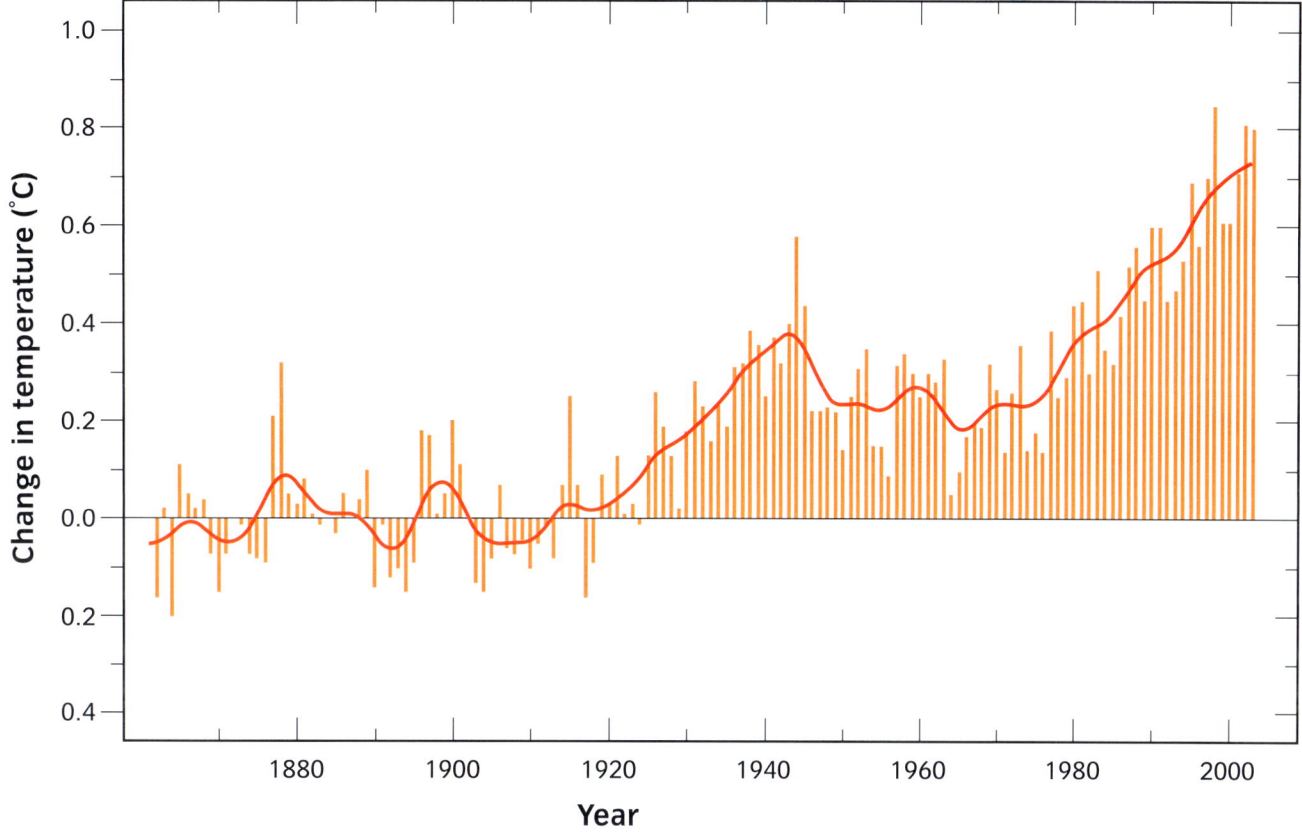

● **Figure 2** Annual mean global surface air temperature, 1860–2000

Therefore, the way we think about climate change depends on our view of it. If we look at only the past 100 years, we might agree with the idea of 'global warming'. If we take a longer view, we can see that the world's average temperature has been rising and falling for millions of years. Although the average temperature has been rising since the last ice age (around 20,000 years ago), it has been rising for no longer than would normally be expected and, if history repeats itself, will fall again.

Think Point

Graphs can be drawn to be misleading! Think about how you might choose the axes of a graph if you wanted to show climate change in a misleading way. What decisions would you need to make?

Make a misleading graph using the fictitious (and exaggerated!) data in the table below. Hint: think carefully about the scale you choose, and the data you select.

Year	2020	2030	2040	2050	2060	2070	2080	2090	2100
Mean temperature (°C)	10.0	10.5	9.5	11.0	9.0	11.5	10.0	13.0	15.0

● **Figure 3** Melting Antartic Ice floes

2.3 The evidence for climate change

You might be surprised to learn that geographers and scientists have been able to produce temperature records going back millions of years. They use the techniques described below to help them work out past climatic conditions.

Pollen analysis

Pollen is produced in great quantities by some plants and does not decay easily. Pollen (and other material) is deposited by the wind, and forms layers in the order in which it falls. Pollen fossils can reveal which plants existed at a particular point in time. This can then tell us about the climate at that time because most plants require a certain type of climate in order to survive. Pollen has been analysed from places such as peat bogs, ocean floors, ice cores and lake beds.

Dendrochronology

By studying the growth rings in tree trunks (dendrochronology), we can work out when the tree was able to grow quickly (in warmer conditions) and slowly (in a cooler climate). The wider the growth ring, the warmer the temperature at the time of the tree's growth.

Ice core and sediment core analysis

By drilling deep into polar ice and into ocean floors, scientists are able to obtain sediments and gases that were deposited several millions of years ago. They can test the chemicals, gases and the physical matter in order to date them and to work out what the climate conditions were like when they were laid down.

● **Figure 1** Growth rings in tree trunks help scientists to understand our climate

Landscape

The landscape contains much evidence to prove that the climate was previously very different. For example, U-shaped valleys, which were cut by glaciers in much colder climatic conditions, are found in many British upland areas. On coasts, landforms such as raised beaches and rias (drowned valleys) show that sea levels were once different from today's.

● **Figure 2** A U-shaped valley formed by glaciers in Norway

● **Figure 3** The Thames ice fair, 1683 – a historical record of the climate

Historical records

These include: simple weather observations (where basic information about temperature, precipitation and other weather conditions is noted in a continuous record by geographers, amateur weather enthusiasts, etc.); records and diaries of events that are influenced by the weather, such as the dates birds migrate, records of floods and storms; and changes in the dates particular plants flower. Historical records are not always written – there are paintings and sketches, for example, of an 'ice fair' on the River Thames in London during the Little Ice Age, which occurred in 1550–1850. However, historical records are dependent on people making them, and they only give us information about the past few hundred years.

Geological patterns

The 'rock record' is a powerful piece of evidence. By looking at the structure of the rocks below the earth's surface, geographers and geologists can tell what the climate conditions were like when they were laid down. Some rocks and soils can only form in warm climates, others in desert conditions, while glacial deposits are evidence of a very cold period.

Think Point

From the methods listed above, which do you think provides the most reliable source of information about past climates?

Think Point

Do you think the 'hard' scientific evidence from ice cores is any more useful than the 'soft' evidence from diaries and paintings? Why do you think this?

Learning Point

Before we continue, let's check that you understand:
- the difference between weather and climate
- what the expression 'climate change' means
- how the earth's mean temperature has changed over time (both in the long term and more recently)
- how geographers know that climate change has taken place
- why some graphs can be misleading than others.

2.4 Explaining climate change 1: natural causes

Geographers often divide the causes of climate change into two groups: natural changes, and those caused by people. Physical geographers and climatologists are not certain about the causes of climate change. They offer ideas – known as theories – based on research. In this section, we will look at the natural causes of climate change.

Most of the earth's energy comes from the sun. It is the differences in heat from the sun – known as incoming solar radiation, or insolation – that causes the different climates on earth.

In general, the stronger the incoming solar radiation, the warmer the climate will be. Some parts of the earth receive more radiation than others, and so different places on earth have different climates. Radiation, therefore, varies over *space*. It also varies over *time* – the earth receives varying amounts of heat from the sun over a long period.

Below are some of the natural factors that may affect the amount of heat received by the earth.

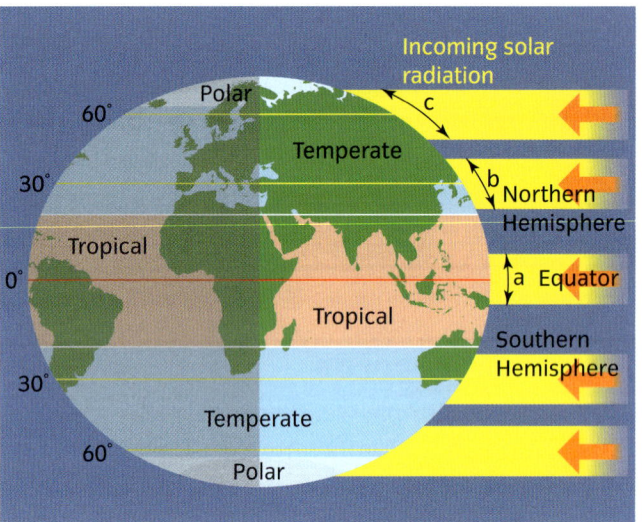

● **Figure 1** The differences in incoming solar radiation cause different climate zones on earth – radiation at (c) is spread over a much greater surface area than at (a)

Sunspots

These are cooler areas on the surface of the sun – they give off less radiation (heat) than other areas of the sun's surface. Where the earth's orbit brings it into alignment with a sunspot, the earth as a whole receives less radiation, and so the earth's climates cool down.

Interstellar material

Radiation from the sun travels up to 150 million kilometres through space before it reaches the earth. On its journey, radiation passes through interstellar material, which consists of gases (99 per cent) and clouds of grains and dust (solid particles) (1 per cent). The clouds of solid particles are dense, and scatter the radiation travelling from the sun. This means that if the radiation passes through unusually dense interstellar material, the earth's incoming solar radiation is reduced and mean temperatures fall.

Irregular orbit

The earth's orbit around the sun is not circular. It is elliptical, which means that at some times it is closer to the sun than at others. In addition, the earth's elliptical orbit changes over time – in a cycle of around 100,000 years. At its maximum, the ellipse is stretched even further than it is today, which means that the contrast between the seasons is greater and varying amounts of solar energy reach the earth.

Dust clouds

Once the incoming solar radiation reaches the atmosphere, its progress towards the earth can be blocked by dust and sand in the air, which can be caused by volcanoes erupting, or sand being eroded and transported by the wind. A volcanic eruption (such as Mount St Helens in 1991) can have a cooling effect on the earth's climate for at least five years afterwards.

The greenhouse effect

Imagine a greenhouse: energy (in the form of radiation) arrives and passes through the glass panels. It begins to heat the surfaces (particularly the darker ones) inside the greenhouse, which become hot and begin to warm the air above them. The warm air rises and reaches the greenhouse roof, but it cannot escape through the glass, and so the greenhouse becomes gradually warmer. The 'greenhouse effect' on a global scale is shown in Figure 2. The layer of greenhouse gases (which includes carbon dioxide, methane, nitrous oxide and water vapour) acts like a blanket around the earth, keeping it artificially warm. Without the greenhouse gases, the earth's climates would be around 30°C cooler on average – and human life could not exist.

Action Point

Draw a single diagram to represent all the natural causes of climate change. You may wish to do some further research, perhaps on the Internet, to get more information. Make sure that the diagram is fully labelled and has a clear title.

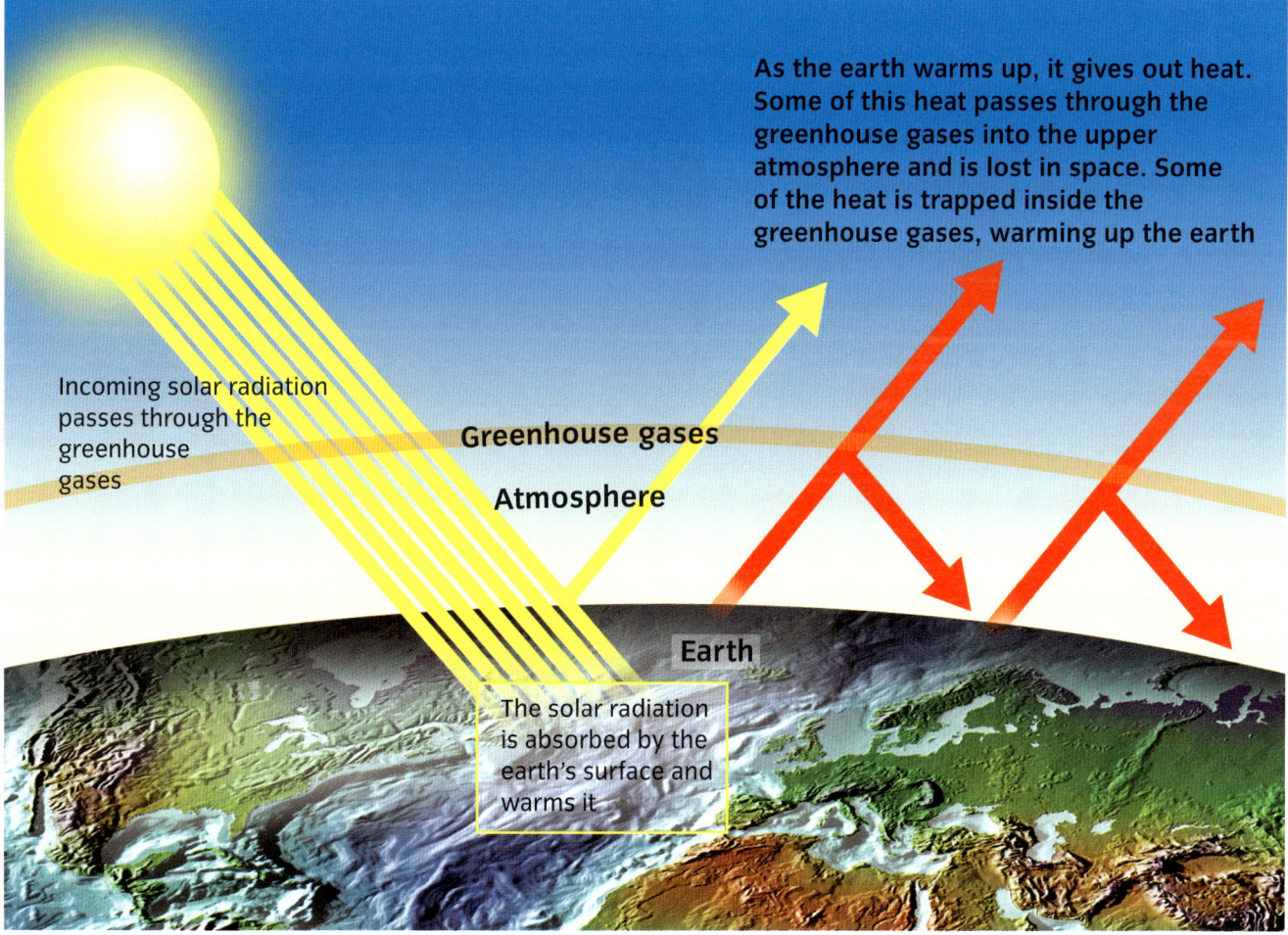

● **Figure 2** The greenhouse effect

2.5 Explaining climate change 2: human causes

Some scientists argue that the earth has warmed up so significantly over the past 40 years that natural explanations are insufficient. They suggest that human activity is responsible for an increase in the quantity of greenhouse gases that blanket the earth, which means that heat has more difficulty in escaping the earth's atmosphere. In short, it seems that people are adding to the greenhouse effect by releasing particular gases into the atmosphere. This is known as the 'enhanced greenhouse effect'.

There are a number of different ways in which people's activities release greenhouse gases into the atmosphere.

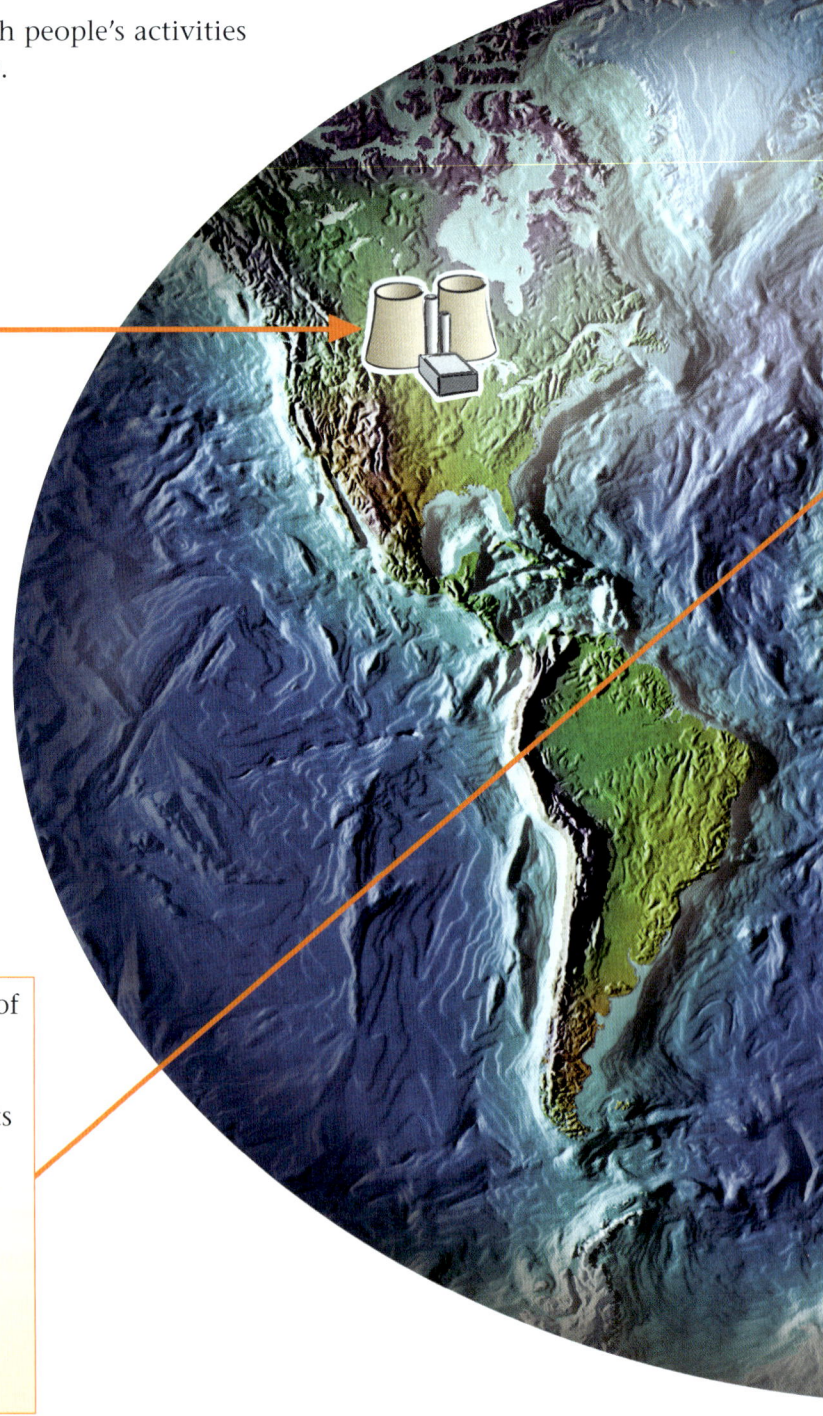

Burning fossil fuels. Gas, oil and coal are fossil fuels and consist mainly of carbon. When they are burned, they release the greenhouse gas carbon dioxide (CO_2) into the atmosphere.

Nitrous oxide. One of the largest sources of nitrous oxide is agriculture. Many farmers use large quantities of fertiliser, which contains nitrates, on their soil to improve its productivity. This releases the gas nitrous oxide (N_2O). Other sources of nitrous oxide include clothing manufacturing processes and the increasing numbers of catalytic converters fitted to cars (which reduce the emission of other poisonous gases such as carbon monoxide (CO)).

Halocarbons. These are very powerful greenhouse gases. They do not generally occur naturally but are manufactured by people. The most common example is CFCs (chlorofluorocarbons) which, until 1987, were used as a cooling gas in fridges and as a propellant in aerosol cans. Even though their use has been reduced, CFCs can remain in the atmosphere for 400 years. They are very effective at trapping heat inside the atmosphere. The use of some halocarbons remains unrestricted.

Methane. People's demand for rice and dairy products is quite high, but the fields in which rice is grown give off large quantities of methane (CH_4). Cows also emit methane.

Think Point

There are many natural causes of climate change. From the scientific evidence found in ice cores and ocean-floor sediments, geographers and scientists know that the earth's climate has changed dramatically since 850 million years ago. Given that people have been living on the earth for less than 3,000 of those years, and seriously polluting it for only the last 200, should we assume that climates will continue to change naturally?

2.6 Consequences of climate change

It is predicted that climate change over the next 100 years will see the world's mean temperature rise. How much it will rise, and how quickly, is a matter of debate. The estimates of the Hadley Centre (part of the Met Office that researches climate change) are shown in Figure 1.

The predicted increase in temperature is likely to have consequences for people and the environments in which they live. In Europe, the European Environment Agency predicts temperature increases of 2.0–6.3°C before the year 2100.

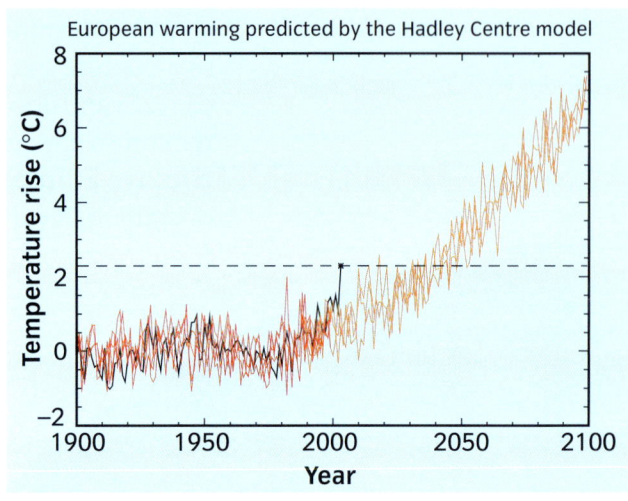

Figure 1 The Hadley Centre predicts a rise in temperatures in Europe over the next 100 years

These are the likely effects of climate change on the northern hemisphere:

- Patterns of rainfall will change. Central and northern Europe are likely to receive more rainfall, whereas south and south-east Europe are likely to become drier. The same effect is expected within Britain – the north may become wetter, and the south and south east drier. This may cause droughts and more frequent crop failures. Where rainfall levels rise, flooding events will become increasingly frequent and severe.
- Europe's glaciers will begin to melt rapidly. Rivers through which the meltwater escapes may rise rapidly, and increased flooding is likely.
- Sea levels will rise globally because of melting polar ice. For Europe, this means that low-lying land (such as parts of the East Anglian coast) may be lost to the sea.
- Plant species will gradually move (migrate) northwards as the climate changes. However, some species (such as hardwood trees) will find it more difficult to migrate than others. Some species will become extinct as a result, although species new to Europe will arrive from the south.
- An increase in levels of carbon dioxide is likely to improve the growth of crops, because it is an important nutrient for plants, particularly where temperatures rise and water is available to meet the plants' increased requirements.
- The water levels in rivers are likely to change. The **rate of discharge** in north and north-east Europe is likely to rise (as rainfall increases), but south and south-east Europe will see discharge fall. This means that the availability of water to people will change within Europe. Some warmer, drier parts of Europe may begin to see increasingly frequent and severe droughts.

Think Point

Using an atlas, find Europe's glaciers. Which rivers would be affected by increased discharge? What problems might this cause, and where?

- There will be an increase in the number of extreme weather events such as storms and hurricanes. Floods, such as those in Boscastle in Cornwall in 2004, will become more commonplace.

- **Figure 2** Flooding in Boscastle, 2004

Think Point

Investigate what caused the flash flood in Boscastle. What were the consequences for people and buildings? If you have access to the Internet, you may be able to find some images to help your answer.

- The rise in mean temperatures will lead to an increase in diseases spread by insects, such as the mosquito, as they move north with the warmer temperatures.
- The ocean current that keeps Britain's climate relatively warm – the North Atlantic Drift – may be interrupted. The interruption may be caused by millions of litres of fresh water from melted polar ice moving south, and colliding with the North Atlantic Drift. If this were to happen, the effects on Britain's climate could be dramatic, with noticeable falls in mean temperatures. However, oceanographers and climatologists disagree about the likelihood of such an event.

Think Point

In pairs, plot each of the likely consequences of climate change listed above on a blank map of Europe. Use colours where necessary and arrows to show movements. Make sure that your map is fully labelled and clearly titled.

Learning Point

Before we continue, let's check that you understand:
- the difference between natural and human causes of climate change
- what the natural causes of climate change are
- why some of the causes of climate change are beyond the control of people
- what the human causes of climate change are.

2.7 The climate change debate

Climate change is one of the biggest geographical issues today. It is having an impact on the world's physical geography, which in turn will have an effect on people and therefore on human geography.

There are many different groups of people taking part in the climate change debate. They include governments, politicians, scientists (climatologists and others) and environmental pressure groups such as Greenpeace. However, not everyone agrees that people are causing climate change, and some think that climate change is not necessarily a problem for people to solve. As geographers, our job is to try to understand not only the causes and the consequences of global warming but also the viewpoints of the people in the debate. Below are some of those viewpoints.

> 'Are humans causing the climate to change? By most accounts, man-made emissions have had no more than a tiny impact on the climate. Although the climate has warmed slightly in the last 100 years, 70 per cent of that warming occurred prior to 1940, before the rise in greenhouse gas emissions from industrial processes.' (Dr R. C. Balling, Arizona State University)
>
> *– The Cooler Heads Coalition*

> 'For more than a century, people have relied on fossil fuels such as oil, coal and gas for their energy needs. Now, worldwide, people and the environment are experiencing the consequences. Global warming, caused by burning fossil fuels, is the worst environmental problem we face today.'
>
> *– Greenpeace*

> 'The scientific evidence is growing that man-made greenhouse gas emissions are having a noticeable effect on the earth's climate. Globally, the ten hottest years on record have all occurred since the beginning of the 1990s. Current climate models predict that global temperatures could warm from between 1.4 to 5.8°C over the next 100 years, depending on the amounts of greenhouse gases emitted and the sensitivity of the climate system. The social, environmental and economic costs associated with this could be huge.'
>
> *– UK government*

Think Point

Summarise each of the three viewpoints using your own words.

What examples can you find of persuasive writing and bias in the three viewpoints? Why do you think each has been written in the way that it has?

Based on your understanding of climate change so far, write a short piece in a form of your choice, such as a newspaper article, poem, song, email, text message or blog to express your own views.

2.8 Is there a solution to climate change?

Many people agree that we must take action to try to alter the course of climate change. However, many of the factors that control climate change cannot be influenced by people in any way. For example, we cannot change the earth's orbit, its alignment with the sun's surface or the solid material that scatters incoming radiation before it reaches the earth's atmosphere.

What can be influenced, though, is the 'greenhouse effect'. This is where people release greenhouse gases into the atmosphere, over and above those that occur naturally.

There are many groups of people taking action to address the issue of climate change. Here are just a few examples:
- governments acting alone and working jointly with other governments
- environmental pressure groups such as Greenpeace
- companies like the Carbon Trust
- individual people like you and your families.

Kyoto: an example of joint action by governments

More than 160 of the world's governments met in the Japanese city of Kyoto in 1997 to discuss climate change. After difficult negotiations, and much disagreement, the outcome was the Kyoto Protocol – an agreement to reduce (with some exceptions) each participating country's emissions of six greenhouse gases. The targets set in Kyoto have been adopted by 110 governments worldwide, although many developing countries (such as China) and the world's largest polluter (the USA) have refused to sign the protocol.

Figure 1 Not all sources of pollution can be prevented. This image shows forest fires in central America in 2003

● **Figure 2** A house in Oxford using 'green energy'

The UK: planning for a different climate

The UK government is taking action in the light of the changing climate. There is a gradual move towards renewable energy, such as wind power and solar power, and away from fossil-burning power stations. This will reduce carbon dioxide emissions but will also change people's behaviour as they switch to suppliers of 'green energy'.

The government is also encouraging people to switch to 'greener' types of transport. 'Green transport' involves people using buses, bikes and trains instead of their cars. At the same time, research is being carried out into cleaner fuels to replace 'dirty' fuels like petrol and diesel.

Work has begun on predicting climate change in order to assess the likely changes to our everyday lives. Figure 1 shows predictions for future temperature and rainfall based on the work of the UK Climates Impact Programme (UKCIP).

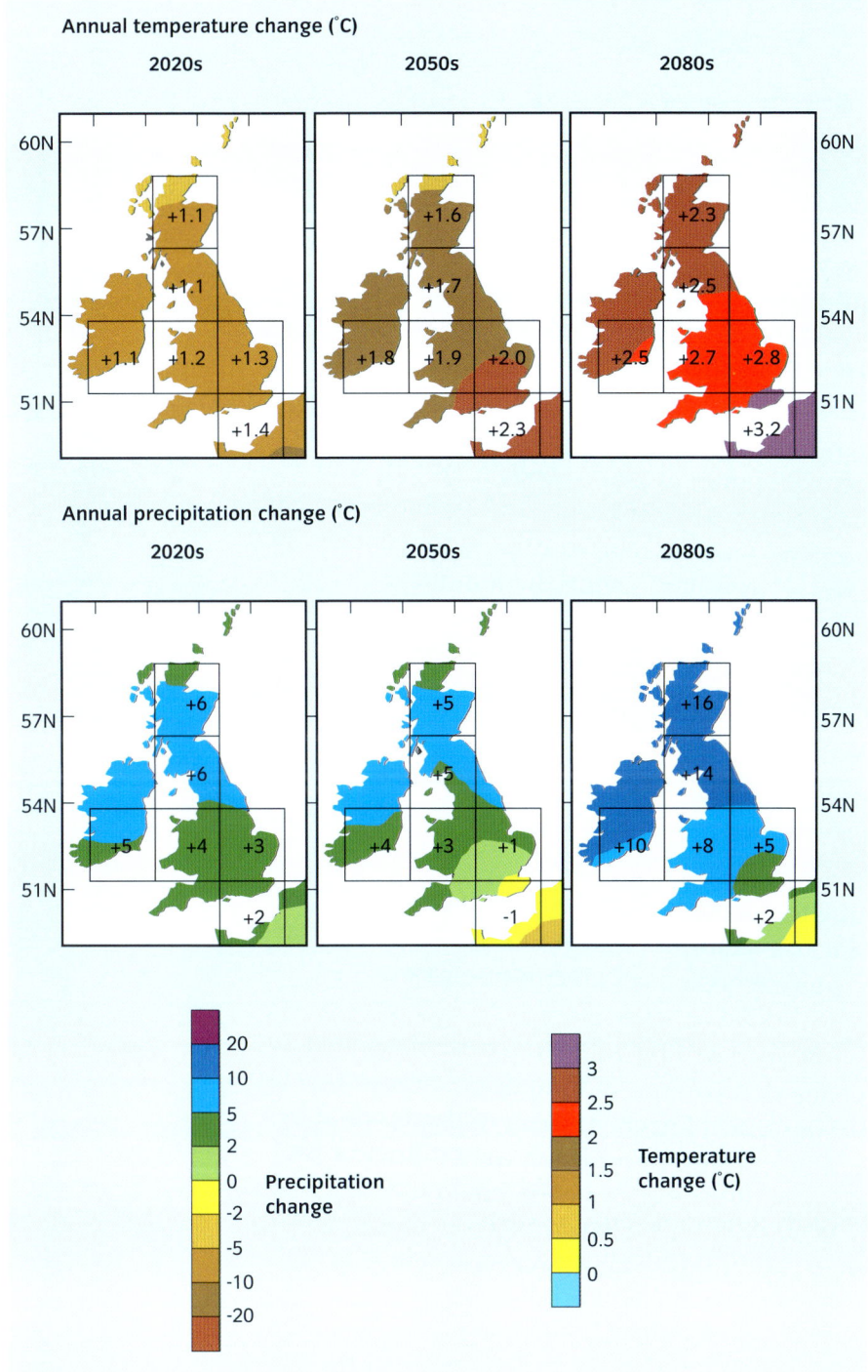

● **Figure 3** Predicted changes in annual temperature and rainfall for the 2020s, 2050s and 2080s
Source: Climatic Research Unit, Oxford

What can individuals do?

It is very easy to leave decisions and actions to other people. However, if we all did that, no action would ever be taken! Many families take small, but important, steps towards reducing their energy consumption, such as turning off lights in empty rooms, and ensuring their homes are properly insulated. They save money, and may make a difference to future climate change.

Think Point

Look at Figure 3. Which places do you think will be affected the most by climate change? Which is likely to be affected the least? How will they be affected? Make a note of the reasons for your decisions.

If you were a member of the UK government, would you take action to help some parts of the country? The Department for Food, Environment and Rural Affairs website may help you in your work. Go to www.heinemann.co.uk/hotlinks, enter the express code 031XP and click on the link. Try to use other sources too.

Action Point

Investigate the steps people can take to reduce their energy consumption and which may, in turn, affect climate change. First, hold a class or group brainstorm to give you some ideas. Use the Internet or your school or local library to help you.

Think Point

Look again at the diagram showing your ideas on global warming and climate change that you drew at the beginning of the chapter. How have your ideas changed?

Assessment

Communication is a vital skill for geographers. In this assessment, you will be asked to practise your communication skills, and also to work independently on developing your knowledge and understanding of climate change.

Your task is to design a leaflet or a PowerPoint presentation. The audience is the parents of pupils at your school. Your aim is to persuade them to take action in their homes and businesses to reduce their energy consumption – which may contribute to reducing the effects of climate change, as well as saving them money!

Your leaflet or presentation should include the following:

- a clear explanation of the natural and the human causes of global warming
- information about the likely effects of climate change on people
- your opinion on whether people can influence climate change, and the reasons for your opinion
- persuasive writing to encourage parents to reduce their energy consumption. Include examples of what they might do to save money and to reduce emissions of greenhouse gases.

Remember to support your writing with diagrams. Make your writing clear – assume that parents and pupils are new to this topic. You could improve your own knowledge and understanding by researching more widely: think about using the Internet or the library for more sources of information. You could try the Atmosphere, Climate and Environment (ACE) website: go to www.heinemann.co.uk/hotlinks, enter the express code 031XP and click on the link.

Chapter 3

Planning in Britain

3.1 The built environment
3.2 Victorian London
3.3 The garden city
3.4 The New Towns
3.5 Planning at the national level
3.6 Planning at the regional level
3.7 Planning at the local level
3.8 The Coin Street community

3.1 Planning the built environment

Look at the environment around you. It's likely to be familiar, and you probably take it for granted – but what you see in the landscape is not fixed. The environment in which you live has changed in the past, is changing now and will continue to change in the future. Think about recent changes in your area – perhaps new houses or a shopping centre have been built, or the use of the countryside has changed from farming to leisure uses. Changes in our landscape, whether built or rural, do not happen by accident – they are almost always planned. This chapter is about planning – the way in which changes in our environment are designed and controlled.

● **Figure 1** These new houses will change the landscape

In Britain, change happens through a planning system, which is controlled by national government (that is, Parliament and the Scottish and Welsh Assemblies) and local government (the local authority in your area). People who want to change the use of the land, or to build new buildings, must apply to the government for planning permission. If permission is not given, the change cannot take place.

As geographers, we are interested in planning because it helps us to understand why the built environment is like it is today. Looking at the development plans of local authorities will also help us to understand how places may change in the future.

Action Point

Look through some local newspapers and/or at websites. Write about the ways in which you think your local area is changing. Use examples and, if possible, include some maps in your answer.

Car plant shuts with loss of 6,000 jobs

Council set to approve business park plans

High-tech business park proposed for former car plant site

● **Figure 2** The built landscape is changing all the time

Our starting point for understanding planning, though, should be in the past. So, let's take a look at Victorian Britain where the need for planning was first realised.

3.2 Victorian London

Britain's towns and cities have changed over time. Although some parts of today's urban areas are more deprived than others, and some people in Britain still live in poverty, on the whole our quality of life has improved greatly over time. Living and working conditions in Victorian Britain were far less pleasant than they are today.

Victorian London, for example, contained many areas of poverty. Many people had moved to London in the hope of finding work. They came from the countryside, where unemployment was rising rapidly because fewer jobs were needed in agriculture. So many people migrated to London that the city was unable to cope. Waste disposal was very poor, water supplies were scarce, polluted and carried diseases such as cholera, and there were few medical facilities. Many people lived in squalor and the life expectancy of both adults and children was very short.

Between 1886 and 1903, the Victorian **philanthropist**, Charles Booth, set up an inquiry into poverty, industry and religion in London. One of the results of the inquiry was a series of maps of London. Booth's maps represent his findings over space. He divided people into seven categories, or social classes – the maps are colour coded to show where the people in each of these groups lived (see Figure 1).

Today's London is very different from the one Booth knew. Although there are some poor areas, the poverty of Booth's day is long gone. Planning led to a major improvement in living conditions, not only in London but also in towns and cities across Britain.

Think Point
Why do you think people continued to migrate to London in vast numbers, despite its very poor living conditions?

Think Point
What do you think about the categories Booth used to classify London? Were they suitable then? Do you think they would still be suitable today?

Action Point
Using Figure 1, what do the Booth maps tell us about the geography of Victorian London? Try to make five different points, using evidence or examples in your answer.

● **Figure 1** Booth's map of East London

3.3 The garden city

Building new cities in the countryside – garden cities – was the idea of Sir Ebenezer Howard (1850–1928). His work still influences geography and our built environment.

Howard wanted to solve the problem of London's overcrowding. His revolutionary idea was to build brand new cities in the countryside, which would combine the advantages of living in a city with the benefits of living in the countryside. He believed that people would be attracted to these garden cities and so move out of the overcrowded Victorian cities. This was one of the first examples of planning in Britain.

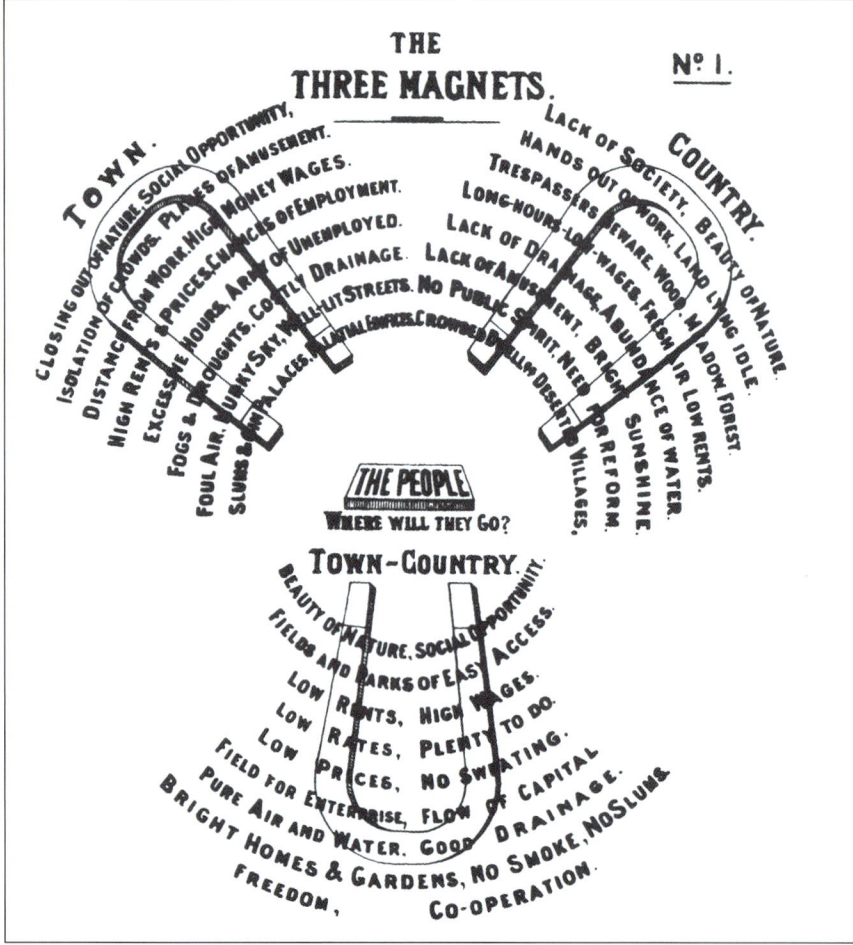

● **Figure 1** Howard's 'Three Magnets' diagram lists the advantages of the new 'town-country' settlements

Think Point

Using Figure 1, list the advantages of town-country settlements, compared with living in the town or the country.

Howard's garden city involved moving 250,000 people out of London into the country. There was to be one central city (housing 58,000 people) surrounded by a circle of six smaller cities, each housing 32,000 people. Everywhere was to be connected to everywhere else by road, railway and canal, which would keep travelling distances between jobs, houses and leisure activities to a minimum. Howard had planned for **interdependence** and **sustainability** 100 years before today's geographers started to use these terms.

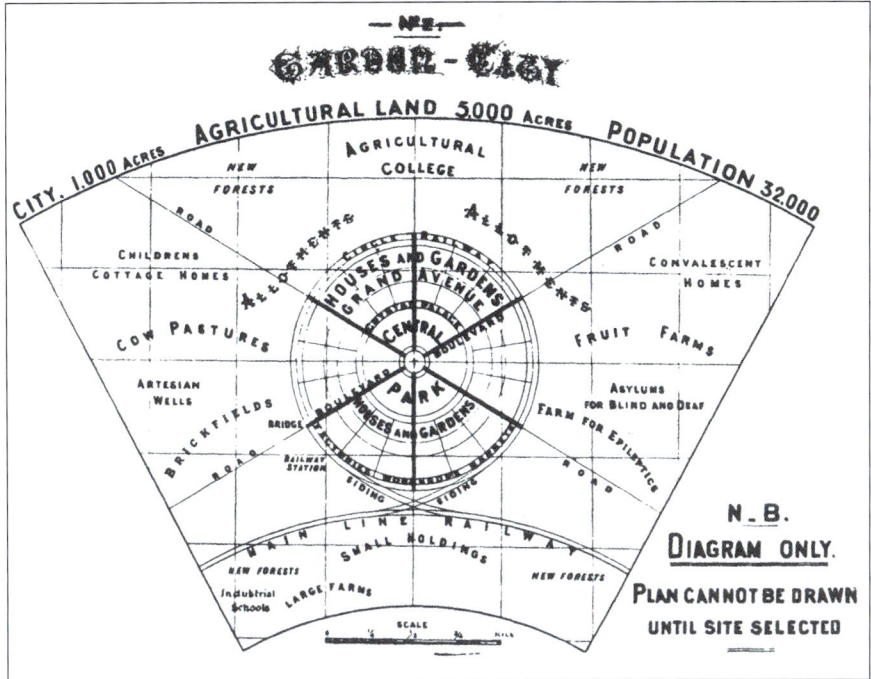

● **Figure 2** Howard's plan of one of the smaller cities in his garden city idea

Each of Howard's garden cities was to be surrounded by green belt – this was land on which building was prohibited. Therefore, the garden city would not be allowed to sprawl, like almost every British town and city has since. Once it had 32,000 residents, it was full, and the next garden city would be built.

Only two garden cities were built – Letchworth and Welwyn Garden City, both in Hertfordshire – but Ebenezer Howard's ideas have had a major influence on today's geography. They formed part of the New Towns Act 1946, which led to the building of 28 New Towns across England, in which 2.25 million people live today.

Think Point

Why do you think Howard wanted to surround the garden cities with green belt? Should settlements be allowed to expand horizontally or vertically as they grow? Or should they not be allowed to expand at all?

Action Point

Write about Ebenezer Howard's garden cities idea. Try to include points in favour of the cities, and points against. (If you can, find out some more information about the garden city, either using a library or the Internet.) Do you think the garden cities were a good idea? Include your own views on Howard's work.

● **Figure 3** Letchworth Garden City

3.4 The New Towns

Since 1946, 32 New Towns have been built in the UK. Today, more than 2.5 million people live in New Towns – over one million of them have moved out of increasingly overcrowded cities. The New Towns had two aims:

- To improve people's living and working conditions.
- To ease the pressure on older, crowded cities.

One example of a large New Town is Milton Keynes in Buckinghamshire. With a population of around 220,000, the town has grown rapidly since it was designated as a New Town in 1967. It was built to take up the overspill of population from London and ease pressure on the Buckinghamshire countryside. It took in the railway towns of Wolverton and Bletchley as well as a number of smaller towns and villages.

Think Point

Look at the location of the New Towns shown in Figure 1. What patterns do you notice?

● Figure 1 New Towns in the UK

● Figure 2 The location of Milton Keynes

English Partnerships, the government body responsible for the New Towns in England, believes that Milton Keynes is one of the most successful New Town developments.

Milton Keynes – a success story

● **Figure 3** Pennyland Basin, Milton Keynes

With an area of 8,900 ha (22,000 acres), Milton Keynes enjoys a strategic location, impressive design, first-class industrial and commercial premises and an excellent quality of life. In recent years, Milton Keynes has undergone a major leisure and growth expansion, including the opening of the first UK real indoor ski slope complex, Xscape, and a further development of some 50 shops in the main shopping centre – Midsummer Place.

Travel and transport. Milton Keynes is well placed for major cities including London, Birmingham, Cambridge and Oxford. It has a fast rail link into London Euston (approximately 45 minutes).

Employment. Milton Keynes is the business base for more than 3,500 companies. Main industries in the area include electronics, computing, financial services, food processing, distribution and business services. Major employers include the Open University, Argos and Tesco.

Leisure. There is no shortage of green spaces with 4,500 acres of river valleys, woodlands, lakesides and parks. The city has well over 20 million trees.

Source: the English Partnerships website

Think Point

As geographers, we need to be aware that information may be biased. Do you think there is any bias in the passage about Milton Keynes? Support your answer with evidence from the text.

Action Point

What might be the advantages and disadvantages of living in a New Town like Milton Keynes? Write a paragraph on each side of the argument.

Learning Point

Before we continue, let's check that you understand:
- why planning might help us to understand changes to our local area
- what conditions were like in Victorian London
- why planning helped to improve people's quality of life in major cities
- why Ebenezer Howard had a major influence on planning
- why the New Towns were built, and the advantages and disadvantages of living in them?

3.5 Planning at the national level

The built environment includes the places in which we live, work, study and shop – all the places that are central to the geographies of our everyday lives. The planning system in Britain means that no development, or change of land use, can take place without permission from the government, so, as geographers, it is important for us to understand how the planning system works.

Planning in the UK takes place at three levels: national, regional and local (see Figure 1). (The next two sections look at planning at regional and local levels.)

> **Think Point**
>
> What might the built environment be like if there was no planning system?

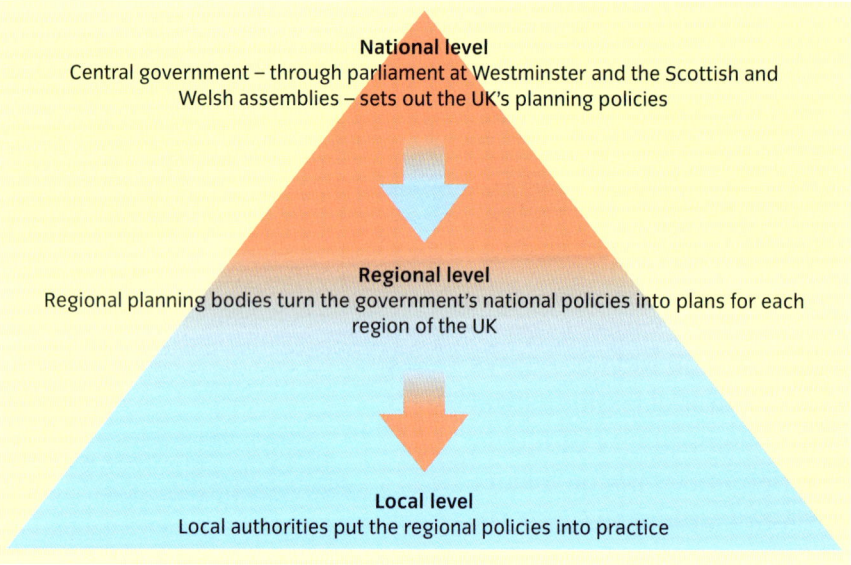

● Figure 1 The three levels of planning in the UK

At the national level, the government is the most important level in the planning process. It is certainly the most influential. This is because it sets national policies that are followed by regional and local planners – in other words, the government makes the planning rules.

The purpose of the British planning system is a complicated one – it attempts to make our environment and quality of life as good as possible, while also helping the economy to be as successful as it can. It therefore has to weigh up the views of many different groups of people such as businesses, developers, local residents and environmental pressure groups like Friends of the Earth.

When deciding planning policies, the government has to take into account several national issues. For example:
- Climate change is likely to require planning for hotter, drier conditions in south-east England (more water supplies may be needed, for example) and for more frequent flooding in other parts of the country.

● **Figure 2** Flooding in York, 2000

- Britain's roads are becoming increasingly congested, because of rising car ownership and people wanting to travel more. The government has to consider whether more road building should take place and how to bring about improvements in public transport.

● **Figure 3** Congestion on Britain's roads

- Supplies of fossil fuels will run out rapidly if they continue to be used as quickly as they are at the moment. This means that alternative sources of energy must be found to supply electricity to Britain's homes and businesses, and fuels other than petrol and diesel will be required to power our vehicles.
- Population is an important issue which is linked to Britain's housing needs. A rapidly rising divorce rate, people with more money to spend, a longer life expectancy and the popularity of Britain as a destination for migrant workers are all factors causing a demand for homes. A key role of national planning policy is to decide where those homes should be built.

Think Point

Try to work out why these issues are considered at a national level rather than at a local level. Can you think of any other national issues that would be best considered nationally rather than locally? Is there an argument for leaving all planning decisions to local planners?

Action Point

Imagine you are an MP preparing to make a speech on planning in your constituency. Think about which major national issues affect the people in the place where you live, for example there may be high rates of unemployment, or serious traffic congestion, or too few affordable houses for local people. Now write your speech, setting out how the government should plan to help your constituency. Be as persuasive as you can.

3.6 Planning at the regional level

While it is central government's job to decide national planning policies, the regional planning bodies are responsible for ensuring the policies are put into practice in each of the UK's regions. The country's regions are varied, both in terms of prosperity and landscape, and so the regional planning bodies each develop their own regional plan.

The West Midlands' plan, for example, aims to 'make the West Midlands a better place in which to live and work', and it includes:

- the amount of housing to be built in different parts of the region
- which city and town centres are to be targeted for economic growth
- where major new areas of employment are needed
- how and where the environment should be improved
- transport priorities.

Figure 1 England's regions

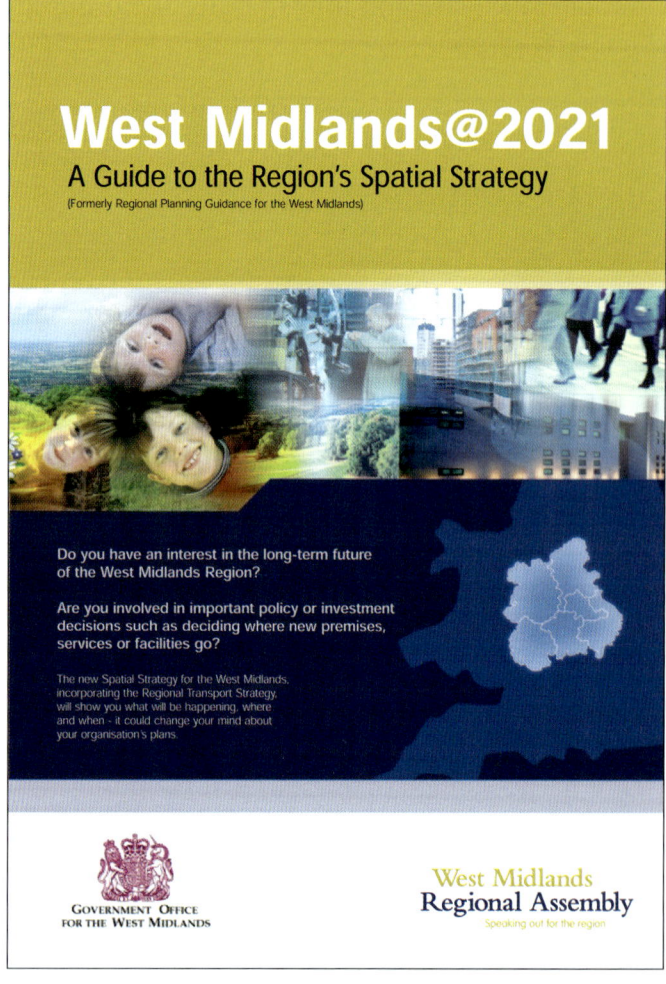

Figure 2 The West Midlands plan gives us information on how the area is likely to change

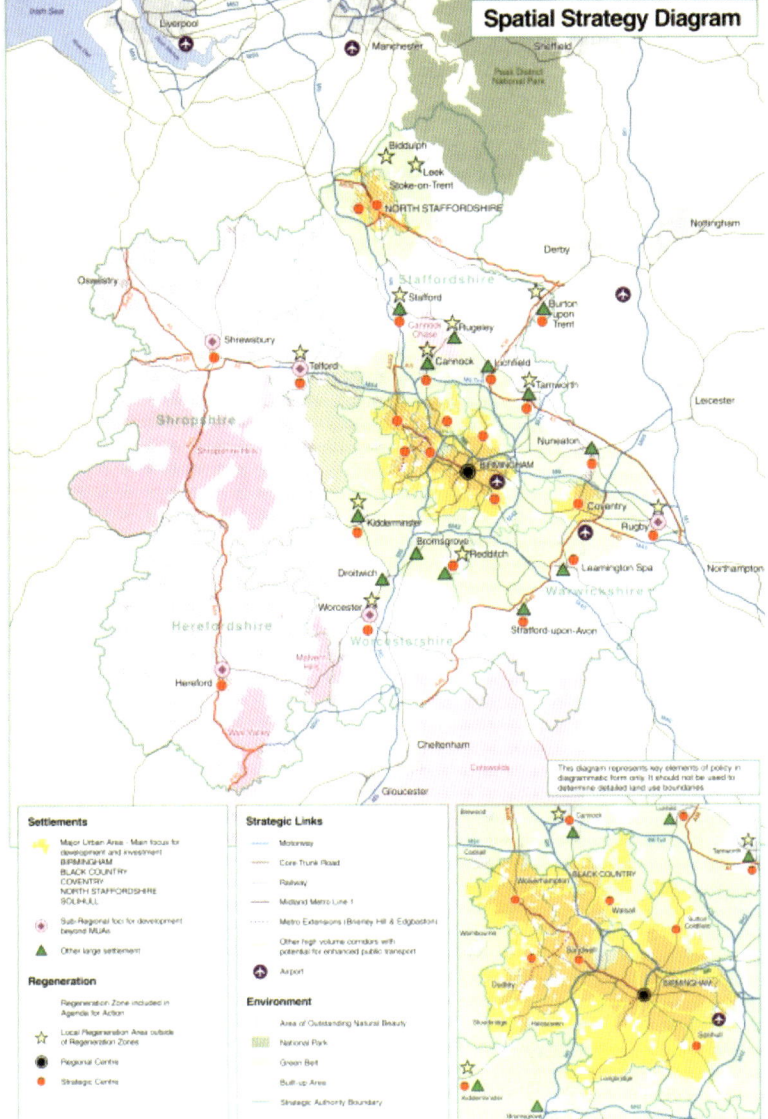

● **Figure 3** The West Midlands' plan covers land use, transport, housing, economic development and the environment

However, it is not the job of the regional planning bodies to put the regional plans into practice at local level. This is done by the local authorities within each region – each local authority takes into account its own area's individual needs. The regional plans are statutory – this means that they are law – and local authorities must therefore follow them.

For our example of the West Midlands, the key planning policies include the following:
- The development and **regeneration** of major urban areas.
- Outside the major urban areas, development is to be focused on five towns (Shrewsbury, Telford, Rugby, Worcester and Hereford) rather than being scattered across the region.
- The regeneration of declining rural areas.
- The development of the region's public transport.

Think Point

What do you think the word 'regeneration' means in geography?

Action Point

Find a copy of the regional plan that covers the area in which you live – your teacher may be able to help with this. They are available on the Internet.

In groups of three or four, investigate how the planners wish your region to change in the future. Write a short summary of where and when changes are due to happen. Next, add your own comments – say whether you think the plan is a good one or not, and the reasons for your opinions.

3.7 Planning at the local level

The job of the local authorities is to put national and regional planning policies into practice. To do this, they write plans – called local development frameworks – to show how they wish their area to develop over time and space. As geographers, this is important to us, because we are interested in how places might change in the future.

Local authorities also have the important job of deciding on planning applications from anyone who wishes to build on, or change the use of, the land – whether it is a house extension or an out-of-town shopping centre. The local authority looks at the planning applications it receives in the light of its local development framework (LDF), and consults people in the area around the proposed development. If the development fits in with the LDF, planning permission is usually given. If many people object, or the application conflicts with the LDF, planning permission may be refused.

One way in which we can predict more accurately how an area might change in the future is to look at the LDF, which includes information such as:

- the local authority's strategic aims (big ideas!) for the area
- the action plan the local authority will follow to achieve its aims, including specific plans for individual places within its area
- how the local authority will include geographical ideas such as **sustainability** and how it will involve the local community in its plans.

Let's look at an example. Birmingham City Council is a local authority – it has to follow the policies set out by the West Midlands Regional Assembly and central government. It does this through its own local development framework. One area for which the Council is responsible is the suburb of Selly Oak, which is situated to the south-west of central Birmingham. Its industry fell into decline 20 years ago, and it is now an area that many people argue is in need of **regeneration**.

Birmingham City Council intends that Selly Oak should change dramatically in the future, and it has published a local plan specifically for Selly Oak. The local authority's planning department will work closely with developers and the local community to try to bring about the changes it has planned.

● **Figure 1** The Selly Oak area of Birmingham

● **Figure 2** A derelict house in Selly Oak

Selly Oak Local Action Plan

The plan sets out a shared vision for Selly Oak which:

- improves and respects the positive character of the plan area
- balances the aspirations of the Selly Oak Community with the wider strategic needs for the new hospital, business park and other major developments
- provides a sustainable framework which allows the City Council to manage and help major development opportunities, in partnership with the community and business
- accommodates change in a positive way.

The plan sets out proposals for:

- improvements to both the built and natural environment
- measures to revitalise Selly Oak shopping centre
- a new road and improvements for pedestrians, buses and cyclists
- the allocation of sites for a new hospital, retail, business, university and residential uses.

Source: the Birmingham City Council website

Action Point

Using the information in the passage on the Selly Oak Local Action Plan, explain in writing how it is planned that the area will change in the coming years. Do you think that the area will change for the better, or worse?

Action Point

Working in pairs, and using a map of your local area, identify a particular development you would like to see take place, such as a new ice rink, or a cinema. Write down what would be built, and where.

Now swap your proposal with another pair's. Imagine you were local planners, would you give planning permission, or not? Write a short report stating clearly your reasons.

3.8 The Coin Street community

The British planning system is an example of top-down planning. This means that the people at the 'top' – the civil servants and politicians of central government (who decide the 'big ideas' of planning in Britain) – have control over the people at the 'bottom' – individuals and companies who put forward planning applications. So, it seems like the people at the top make the rules, and the people at the bottom have to follow them.

However, there are some good examples of 'bottom-up' planning. This is where ordinary people have themselves planned and brought about change in their local area. Sometimes this happens because they have opposed the 'top-down' approach. For example, planners might plan to build many more houses, or to open a large shopping area. If local people were totally opposed to this development, they might put forward plans of their own, which would then be accepted by the planners. This would be an example of bottom-up planning because the end result comes from the 'bottom', rather than the 'top', of the planning system.

> **Action Point**
>
> Draw a diagram of top-down and bottom-up planning. Remember to include labels.

One of the best-known examples of bottom-up planning can be found in the Coin Street area, between Waterloo Bridge and Blackfriars Bridge on the south bank of the River Thames in central London. The 'battle' between the local community and the planners (and developers) began in 1974. The planners had decided that the area, in which many people lived, should be the site of a very large office development. The area's closeness to central London and the Thames meant that the site was worth many millions of pounds to the developers. The problem, however, was that local people objected to being forced from their homes to make way for more office development threatening the loss of shops, schools and other local services.

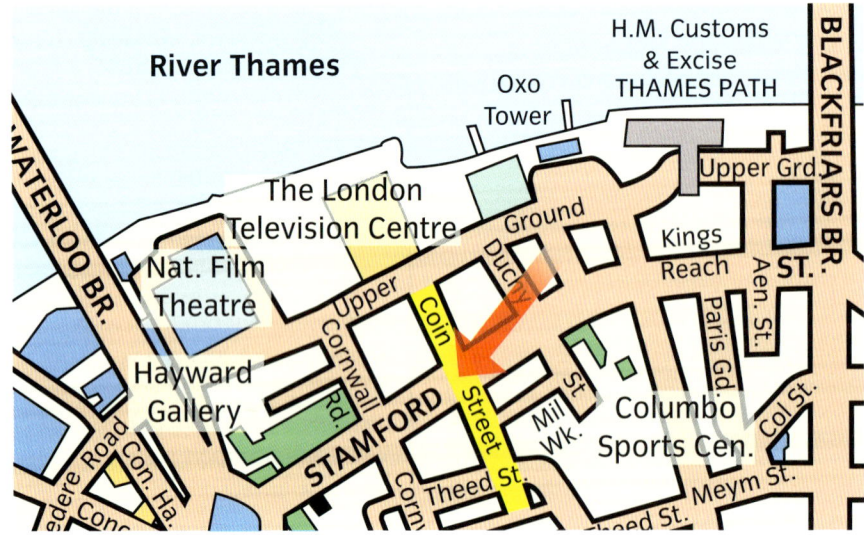

● Figure 1 The Coin Street area

The Coin Street residents instead drew up their own plans for a 'mixed-use' development, which included a variety of different land uses for the area – housing, leisure facilities, a park and space for managed workshops. After a 10-year battle with the developers and planners, they were successful. Known as Coin Street Community Builders, they received planning permission from the local authority for their plans and bought the site.

● **Figure 2** The Coin Street area from the air

● **Figure 3** Community housing in Coin Street

Since 1984, Coin Street Community Builders have transformed the area. In addition, all its profits go towards providing other facilities for the local community that would not otherwise exist. The Coin Street area is well worth visiting if you are able to get to London – it's always good to see real geography in action!

Learning Point

Before we continue, let's check that you understand:
- the three levels of the planning system in the UK, including the differences between them
- why central government decides how to tackle the big issues
- how your own area is planned to change in the future
- the difference between top-down and bottom-up planning.

Think Point

To find out more about Coin Street Community Builders, visit their website. Go to www.heinemann.co.uk/hotlinks, enter the express code 031XP and click on the link.

Action Point

Write about top-down and bottom-up planning. Which do you think might be the better type of planning, or should the planning system somehow try to include both types? Use evidence to support your writing, including as many points as you can on both sides of the argument. Try to come to a clear conclusion at the end of your writing.

Assessment

1. Look back at section 3.3 on Ebenezer Howard's garden cities. It is now more than 100 years since Howard put forward his ideas that changed Britain's geography permanently. With your knowledge of Britain in the twenty-first century, do you think that our quality of life could be improved yet further? If the country looked to you as a 'great thinker', what would be your single best idea to improve the nation's quality of life? Explain your thoughts in detail.

2. Draw a diagram to show the different groups of people local planners have to listen to in order to make balanced judgements. Do you think that some people's opinions are more important than others when it comes to planning your local area? If so, make this clear within your diagram.

3. Using maps of your local area where would you locate the following:
    a   a nightclub
    b   a petrol station
    c   a high-tech business park
    d   a 24-hour supermarket
    e   a sports shop?

You could use a mapping website. Go to www.heinemann.co.uk/hotlinks, enter the express code 031XP and click on the link.
Use six-figure grid references to identify the locations precisely. Remember that you have to balance the needs of local people and businesses. Explain clearly the reasons for your choices.

Chapter 4
Globalisation

- **4.1** What is globalisation?
- **4.2** A shrinking world 1: transport
- **4.3** A shrinking world 2: communications
- **4.4** Joining the world together
- **4.5** Changing places
- **4.6** Global power: countries or companies?
- **4.7** Nike, a global company
- **4.8** Global products, global culture

4.1 What is globalisation?

The word 'globalisation' is often used in newspapers, radio and television, but it is used in so many different ways that it's sometimes hard to know exactly what globalisation means. In fact, there is no single definition of the term 'globalisation' – even geographers disagree about its exact meaning. The aim of this chapter is to make globalisation, a rather complex but very useful geographical idea, much clearer to you.

Let's start by looking at the word itself. 'Global-' means worldwide, and '-isation' suggests a process – in other words, something that happens over time. So we could think of 'globalisation' as being a worldwide process.

Before we try to define globalisation, let's look at two case studies. One is an example of a *product* (Brahma beer), which, already popular within its country of origin, is expanding on a global scale. The second is an example of a *service* (a French TV news channel) expanding across the globe. In geography, we say that both are 'globalising' – both are becoming available to more people by expanding over space.

> **Think Point**
>
> Have you heard the word 'globalisation' before? If so, where did you hear it? In what context was it being used?

Brazil's Brahma beer goes global

Brazil's Brahma beer has for many years been the country's best seller. Now its owners are set to export it worldwide. Brahma is owned by one of the world's biggest brewers, Belgian giant Inbev, which wants to turn the beer into its third main global brand next to Stella Artois and Beck's.

In 2006, Brahma is being sold for the first time in 15 countries, including the UK, USA, Canada, Russia, France, Australia and New Zealand. Inbev says that by the end of 2007 it expects Brahma sales outside of Brazil to be worth £20.5 million a year.

French global news channel ready to launch

France is getting ready to launch its first global, French-language, satellite TV news channel by the end of 2006. French International News Network will initially be available in Europe, Africa and the Middle East. The channel will broadcast news around the clock in French, with some programmes in English.

The French President is keen to see the channel getting across France's views in a global TV news sector dominated by the BBC and the US channel CNN. France 'must be at the forefront of the global battle of images, that's why I am resolved that our country should have an international news channel,' he said.

In geography, globalisation refers to the changes that places and people around the globe are experiencing because the world is becoming better connected. This means that the places and people you know may well be experiencing change because global communication and travel are becoming quicker and easier.

Think Point

Why might companies want to expand their geographical coverage from a smaller scale to a bigger one?

● **Figure 1** Modern technology is enabling globalisation to happen

Action Point

Read the case studies and then write down your answers to the following:
1. Who has decided upon the global expansion of Brahma beer?
2. What do you notice about the countries to which Brahma beer is to be exported? Is there a pattern?
3. What were the French government's motives in launching the French International News Network?
4. Globalisation relies upon improving transport links and communications technologies which make distance much less important. How do the Brahma and French TV news channel case studies rely on such progress?

Chapter 4 Globalisation 51

4.2 A shrinking world 1: transport

Before we look at more examples of globalisation and its consequences, we first need to understand the changes in the world that have led to globalisation. The first is much-improved transport; the second is a revolution in communications.

You may have heard people talking about a 'shrinking world'. This is the idea that the connections between places – roads, railways, air travel, telephone, email, worldwide web, and so on – have been speeded up. For example, the opening of the Channel Tunnel reduced the travelling time between Kent and the Pas de Calais region of France by about a half. Figure 1 shows how much travel times have fallen since the 1500s and how much of the world is now accessible.

> **Think Point**
> Why is the term 'shrinking world' used to describe the speeding-up of long-distance travel?

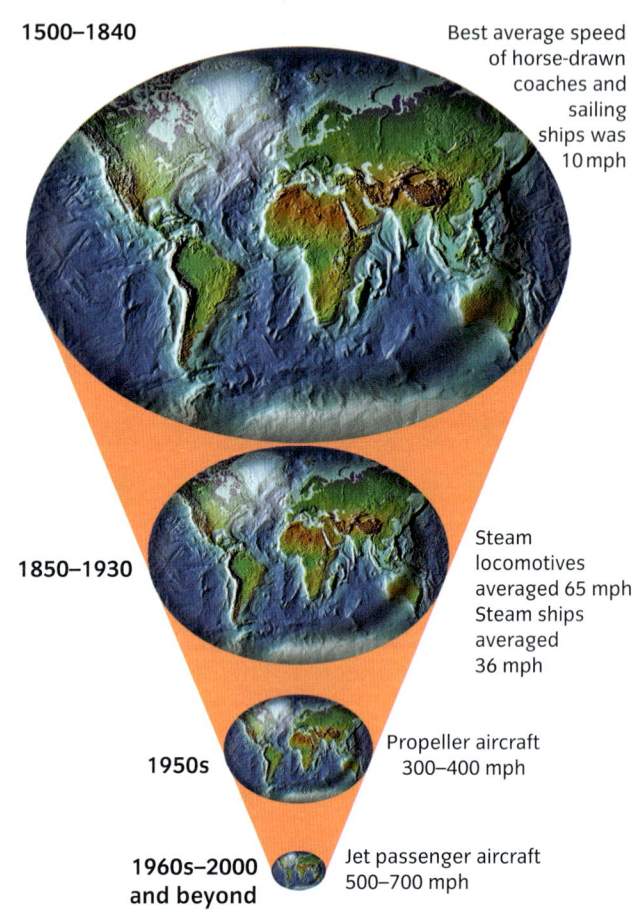

Figure 1 Our shrinking world

By rail and steam: travel in the nineteenth century

In Britain the first real improvements in travelling time came with the coming of the steam railways in the nineteenth century. Journey times were cut considerably and smaller towns and areas suddenly became accessible to the general population. For example, it was the expansion of the railways that enabled coastal towns such as Eastbourne and Newquay to grow into popular seaside resorts.

The improvements in transport had other geographical effects too – it was not until the coming of the railways that clocks in different parts of Britain told the same time!

> **Think Point**
> How do you think people travelled before the coming of the railways?

While travelling times in the UK were getting shorter, the new steamships were speeding up the connections between countries. Ships such as the *SS Great Western* cut the journey time between the UK and the USA by half to 15 days, compared to sailing ships. The speedier international connections provided by steamships led to a major increase in the trade between countries – an early form of globalisation.

By air: travel in the twentieth century

The world continued to 'shrink' during the twentieth century, but through a different type of transport – the aeroplane. From the early flights of the 1920s, the aircraft industry quickly found itself able to fly people around the world at unthought-of speeds. The height of its achievement came in 1976 with the supersonic aircraft Concorde, which reached speeds of 1,350 miles per hour, and was able to connect London and New York in around three hours. One of the few setbacks in the shrinking world came when Concorde was withdrawn from service in 2003 – minimum journey times between London and New York increased to around seven hours.

The airline industry continues to grow very rapidly. Journey times between places are falling as:

- more airline routes connect more places directly
- larger aircraft are being developed that can carry ever larger numbers of people
- there are more planes than ever before
- the airlines are using their aircraft more intensively.

● **Figure 2** The largest aircraft ever built – the Airbus A380 will be able to carry as many as 840 passengers and fly distances of more than 10,000 miles

In geographical terms, the continuing growth of the airline industry means that flows of people and goods can now speed to the other side of the world in less than a day. The airline industry therefore enables the process of globalisation to take place – it 'shrinks' the world in ways other types of transport cannot.

Think Point

Given the rapid growth of the airline industry, what effect do you think this may have on the price of flights? What other effects might there be?

Action Point

1. Produce a table listing the advantages and disadvantages of the growing airline (and airport) industry. Say who you think might be affected the most by each advantage/disadvantage.
2. Use the Internet to investigate some airlines' websites. Do they suggest the airlines are growing? Can you find maps of their networks? What other evidence of globalisation can you find in their websites? (If you have limited Internet access, try to find some advertisements for airlines in newspapers or magazines.)

4.3 A shrinking world 2: communications

In the last section, we learned that people are able to travel around the world more quickly and more easily than ever before, but transport improvements on their own have not brought about all the changes that we associate with globalisation. At the same time, there have been dramatic improvements in communications, and therefore to the quantity and quality of flows of information.

Before the nineteenth century, even the smallest pieces of information could take days or months to travel between places, depending on the distance between them. Today, vast amounts of information can travel around the world in seconds.

The new communications technologies have enabled many people to work from home or on the move. Individuals can keep in touch with colleagues, families, friends and other people almost anytime, anywhere! The growing 'wired world' has brought about changes to people's daily routine, to places themselves and, most of all, to the flows of information between people and places.

> **Think Point**
>
> How do you communicate with your friends using communications technology?

We may think very little about exchanging information between people. Emails, mobile phones, satellite television, text messages and online chat are a growing part of our everyday lives. The new and continuing 'communications revolution' affects our geographies too – people can stay in touch in growing numbers of places, as new technologies spread over space.

People and businesses can now work and communicate increasingly flexibly, and where they are – their physical location – matters less and less. It used to be essential for some businesses to be located near to their customers, or close to other related businesses. But ever-improving communications technologies – combined with transport improvements – mean that they can now be located some distance away.

People are also using the new communication technologies to change the way they work, allowing them to spread geographically to benefit from local advantages such as lower wage rates, or particular expertise. Banks, for example, used to employ many staff in branches in villages, towns and cities, but since the 1990s, many branches have closed, and customers increasingly communicate with their bank online or via call centres. Indeed, advances in technology have meant that many such call centres are now located in other countries where wage rates are much lower, such as India.

● **Figure 1** Video conferencing from a home office

1791 Claude Chappe invents the first telegraph, sending messages between Paris and Lille
1876 Alexander Graham Bell has the first telephone conversation over 30 metres of wire
1861 Telephone cables are laid across Europe and the USA.
1879 L.M. Ericsson invents the first telephone handset combining the receiver and the transmitter
1895 Guglielmo Marconi sends the first wireless message
1899 First radio transmission across the English Channel
1925 First television image
1958 STD (standard telephone dialling) service is introduced in the UK, allowing users to make long-distance calls without the need for a telephone operator
1962 Satelite communications station opens at Goonhilly Downs, Cornwall
1963 Intelsat commercial communications satellite is launched into space
1965 Trans-Atlantic telephone cable is laid
1970 First email is sent
1961 Satellite telephones become available
1979 Mobile telephones are introduced
1981 First personal computer (PC) is built
1983 Compact discs (CDs) are introduced; Microsoft introduces Windows software
1991 The worldwide web is launched

- **Figure 2** A communications timeline: 1791 to 1991

Since 1975, global communication has been revolutionised by technologies such as the mobile phone, satellite television and the Internet, resulting in improved quality, quantity, speed and geographical coverage of world communications. For example, it is now possible to watch news from around the world as it happens, even from the remotest places.

Think Point

How did people send and receive information prior to email and the world wide web?

Action Point

1. Make a list of the many different technologies that enable information to flow around the world. Put your list in descending order of their speed.
2. Which do you think was the most important event on the communications timeline? Give your reasons.
3. How do you communicate with other people? Do you consider yourself to be part of an 'information society'? Write about your own experience of communications.

Learning Point

Before we continue, let's check that you understand:
- the term 'shrinking world'
- the improvements in transport that have brought places closer together
- how today's communication technologies are changing the geography of our everyday lives
- the meaning of globalisation.

Think Point

Think of five things that show globalisation in your own home. How do you think they show globalisation? Discuss your thoughts with others in your class.

4.4 Joining the world together

In Chapter 1 we looked at the importance of 'place' in geography. Globalisation means that those places around the world are now getting better connected. As geographers, we need to think not only about places but also about the links, or connections, between those places.

In geography, when there are active links between places – such as people in Paris buying Italian clothing from Milan – these are called **flows**. The reason geographers study flows is because they help us to explain what places are like, and because they can change the geography of people's lives, as well as the places themselves. Below are some important examples of flows.

- People flow between places. These flows can be over short distances such as a journey to work or school, or longer distances such as flying to a holiday destination abroad. Flows of people also vary over time – some journeys are temporary such as people travelling to and from work, while other journeys, such as those of people moving from one country to another to find work (migrant workers), are longer term.
- Goods flow between people and places. For example, coffee is transported from the warm climates in which it is grown, such as Costa Rica in Central America, to the UK and other markets.
- Services and communications flow between people and places. For example, a person may telephone a bank for information about their account. The call centre that handles the call is likely to be in a distant location, possibly in another country altogether, for example in India.
- Money flows between people and places. The money you spend on clothing or food, for example, flows to a variety of different places in the world – from the original producer, to the companies that transport the goods and finally to the retailer who sells the goods to you.

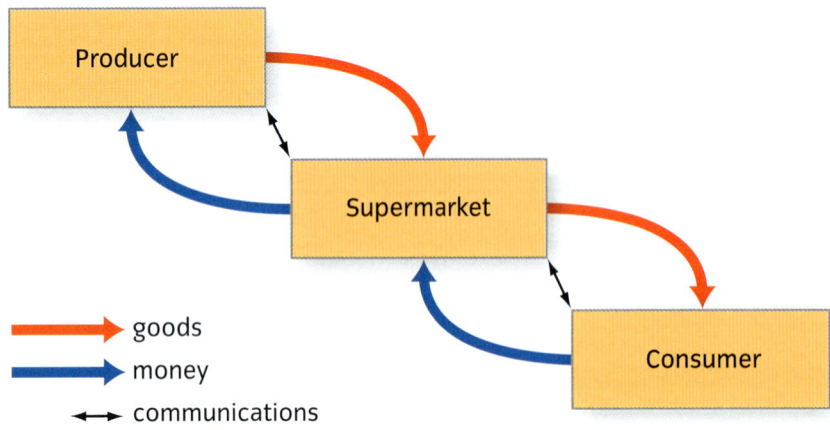

● **Figure 1** Flows of goods, money and communications

● **Figure 2** Goods and money flow between people and places

> **Think Point**
>
> Why do you think that it might be important to study the flows between people and places, and not just places themselves?

In an increasingly globalised world, the distances over which these 'flows' travel become longer and more varied. This is because distance now matters much less to businesses. For example, people in the UK used to buy mainly British-built cars; now, most British people buy cars built in other countries, such as Japan and South Korea, where the costs of production are much lower. Today, very few cars are manufactured in Britain. In this example, globalisation has resulted in:

- customers in the UK being offered competitively priced cars built abroad
- cars travelling much further from the producer (manufacturer) to the customer
- the customers' money flowing abroad rather than to British firms.

Other consequences of globalisation have been the loss of manufacturing jobs in the UK, and a dramatic growth in the car-manufacturing industry in Asia.

> **Think Point**
>
> Why has car manufacturing almost ceased in the UK but is growing rapidly in countries such as China?

Action Point

1. Draw a large diagram to show the flows of people, goods, services, communications and money in and out of your household over a typical month. Label each of the flows.
2. The world is connected by many billions of flows between people and places. Some of the flows are visible, others invisible. Make a table giving examples of visible and invisible flows.
3. Explain whether you think invisible flows are any less important than visible ones. Try to give some examples to support your argument.

Learning Point

Before we continue, let's check that you understand:
- what globalisation involves
- all the different types of flows
- why it is important to study flows, and not just places, in geography.

4.5 Changing places

Although every place is unique, many geographers believe that globalisation can lead to places around the world becoming increasingly similar. They point to the spread of global brands such as McDonald's and Nike, and the spread of western culture to **developing countries** through increased tourism and globally available television channels such as the BBC.

Figure 1 The spread of global brands

Some people argue that places are losing their historic local identities because of globalisation. Town and city centres seem to be particularly affected, where independently owned local businesses have given way to national and global shopping chains such as Next or Starbucks. According to local retailers, this often happens because landlords increase the rent of town-centre shops to levels that only the big brands can afford.

As geographers, we might use the term 'clone town' to describe those places that have lost their local uniqueness more than others.

Think Point

If a town centre became a clone town, do you think its sense of place would change? If so, how?

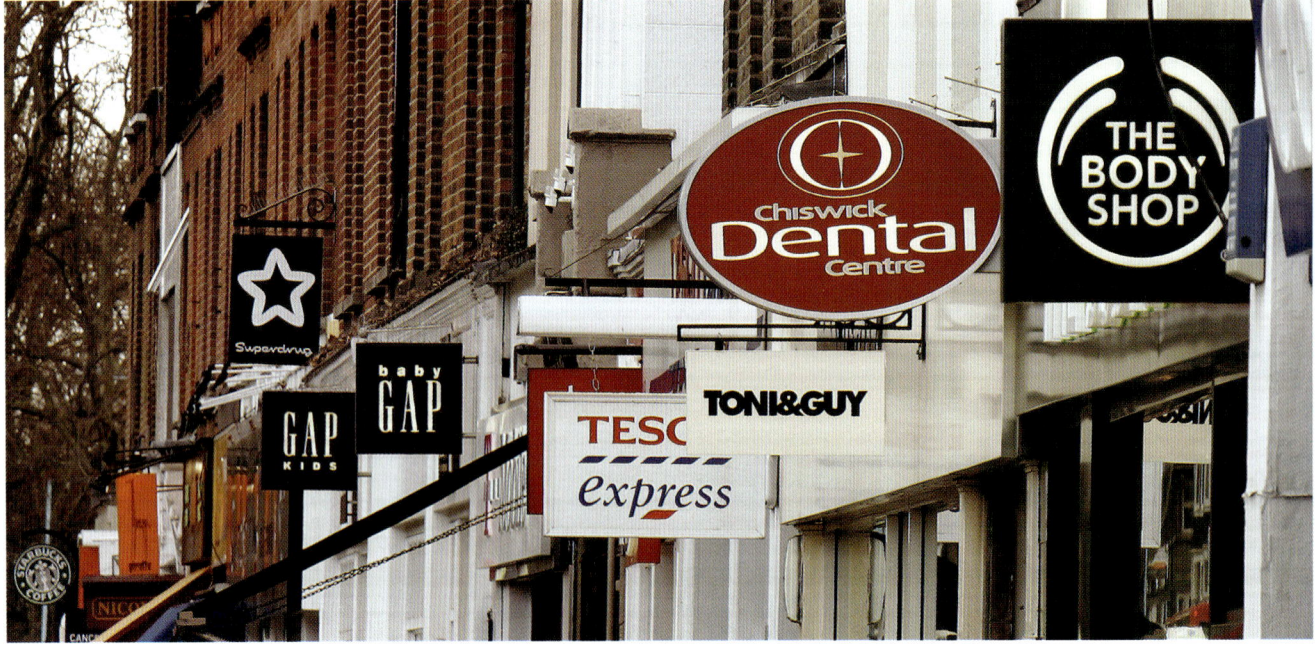

Figure 2 Chiswick: A typical high street in Britain

Retail chains 'cloning' UK towns

Britain's town centres are rapidly losing all sense of local identity as they are taken over by global and national chain stores.

A report from the New Economics Foundation estimated how far the nation's high streets had been taken over by a phenomenon it called 'clone town Britain'. It found 42 of the 103 towns it surveyed in England, Scotland and Wales had become clones, with few local businesses supplied from the surrounding area and a reduced range of specialist outlets.

In these towns, independent butchers, greengrocers, pet shops and dry cleaners had been driven out by national supermarket retailers, fast food chains, mobile phone shops and global fashion outlets. The most extreme example of a clone town was Exeter in Devon, the foundation said. On a scale awarding points for the number of independent outlets and range of specialist shops, it scored 6.9 out of 60.

At the other end of the scale, Hebden Bridge in West Yorkshire scored 48.6. This was the best example of what the foundation called a 'home town' – one retaining its individual character. Inspectors assessed a run of 50 shops in Hebden Bridge and found only three were chain stores.

The foundation said 34 of the 103 high streets it surveyed could still be described as home towns. Another 37 were 'border towns' where colonisation by the clones was not fully established.

Andrew Simms, the foundation's policy director, said: 'Clone stores have a triple whammy on communities. They bleed the local economy of money, destroy the social glue provided by real local shops and steal the identity of our towns and cities. Then we are left with soulless clone towns.'

Source: Adapted from John Carvel, 'Global brands are swamping the individuality of the high streets', *Guardian*, 6 June 2005.

Action Point

Read the newspaper article, 'Retail chains "cloning" UK towns', and remembering what you have learnt from this chapter so far, write down your answers to the following questions.
1. What is the difference between a 'clone town' and a 'home town'?
2. Why does the author feel that globalisation is to blame for the emergence of clone towns?
3. How have high-speed communications and efficient transport systems enabled globalisation to take place?
4. Is there a link between the ideas of a 'shrinking world' and the growth of clone towns? Explain your answer.

4.6 Global power: countries or companies?

Globalisation has allowed businesses to transport goods further and in greater quantities, and to communicate more quickly than ever before. Many companies have taken advantage of cheaper, quicker and better transport networks and almost instant global communication in order to expand geographically, often on a very large scale.

● **Figure 1** McDonald's in Suzhou, near Shanghai, China

● **Figure 2** Countries and major companies, ranked by GDP, 2000

Rank	Country/company
1	United States
2	Japan
…	…
45	ExxonMobil
46	Pakistan
47	General Motors
48	Peru
49	Algeria
50	New Zealand

In section 4.1, we looked at how a Brazilian beer and a French television news station were expanding from their country of origin, but there are better-known examples – think of McDonald's and Sony, both global firms.

When we look at a map of the world, or a globe, it is usually divided up politically – each country is clearly marked. It might be tempting to think that a country's size on the map reflects its influence in the world – its 'global power'. As geographers, we know that this is far from true – some countries on the map, such as Japan, are much more wealthy and influential than others that are much larger in size.

Think Point

Can maps sometimes be misleading? Try to think of some examples.

There are some geographers, though, who argue that individual countries are becoming less important in terms of world power and influence than global companies. Multinational companies, as they are known, are businesses that operate in several countries, such as the oil company Exxon or the software company Microsoft. These geographers argue that the most powerful global companies have much more world influence than some poor countries like Somalia in Africa. For example, if Exxon was thought of as a country, it would be financially more powerful than Pakistan (UNCTAD, 2000).

Multinational companies can create wealth and jobs, invest in places (for example, by opening a new factory) and move resources, such as goods, across the world. They can hire and fire workers on a global scale and influence what is bought and sold in many countries. Very few countries have a similar influence.

As geographers, we need to understand that the main purpose of any company (not just large global ones) is not only to make a profit but to make as much profit as possible. This is usually achieved by keeping costs low and income high.

As a result of ever-quicker and easier communications and better transport links, global companies can spread their activities across the world in order to make as much profit as possible. Companies based in one country can have production centres in other countries where the costs of production are lower. For example, Dyson, the vacuum cleaner manufacturer, has its head office in the UK, while its vacuum cleaners are manufactured in Malaysia.

Think Point

Why do you think that some geographers argue that some of the largest companies have more global power and influence than some countries?

Think Point

What is your opinion about multinational companies employing low-cost labour in countries where wage rates are lowest?

This is also a form of globalisation, but there are geographers who argue that some companies keep their production costs low by employing workers on very low salaries. While this might make sense from a business point of view, some people believe that this takes advantage of the workers, who often work in poor conditions in sweatshops. They campaign in favour of a 'fair wage' for all employees, wherever they are located.

● **Figure 3** Protestors demonstrate against Nike

Action Point

1. How do you think quicker and cheaper transport and communications systems have helped global companies to expand? Suggest at least three ways, using examples where possible. You can find links to the websites of four global companies (Exxon, Microsoft, Nokia and Nestlé) at www.heinemann.co.uk/hotlinks. Enter the express code 031XP and click on the links.
2. On a blank map of the world, use your mapping skills to show the location of three global companies and their sites around the world.

Learning Point

Before we continue, let's check that you understand:
- why some large companies might be more powerful than some countries.

4.7 Nike, a global company

First, let's define what a global company is.

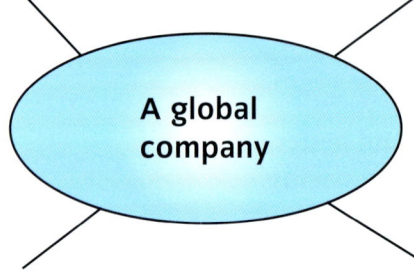

Employs many thousands of people, usually in several countries

Can operate very flexibly – it can launch new products, close factories and open new sites fairly quickly

A global company

Can take advantage of geographical differences in the world (e.g. natural resources in one country; a demand for high-tech products in another country; low-cost workers in another) in order to make as much profit as possible

Has financial power that is often greater than many individual countries

● **Figure 1** Definition of a global company

An example of a global company is the US firm, Nike. Nike describes itself as 'the largest sports and fitness company in the world'.

Some facts about Nike
Nike brand: created in 1971
World headquarters: Oregon, USA
Geographical spread: sales in 120 countries worldwide
Nike employees: 26,000 worldwide
More than 730 factories working for Nike worldwide, employing 650,000 people
Net profit: US $945 million (2004)
Factory workforce: mainly women aged 19–25

Nike does not produce the goods it sells, nor does it sell all of them directly to the public. You could think of it as a 'virtual firm'! Its products are made by factories around the world, mainly in **developing countries** like Asia, where costs are low. These factories do not belong to Nike; the company subcontracts the manufacture of its products to them. Nike then supplies its products to retailers who sell them to the public. What Nike does is run its vast business operation from its headquarters in the USA and, in doing so, it makes huge profits. This is often how global companies work.

● **Figure 2** Nike's products are made in factories such as this one in the Far East

However, in the past, Nike's success story has been criticised by human rights groups, who pointed to the poor working conditions in the factories producing Nike goods. They accused the company of not tackling these problems. Nike's response was to set up a task force in 2005 to look into the low rates of pay, long working hours and poor working conditions.

Investment in poor countries by global companies such as Nike can help to bring about an improvement in people's living standards. Opening factories in developing countries can help to bring jobs and services to these places, which in turn brings more local wealth. Such large flows of money – known as Foreign Direct Investment (FDI) – can help to alter the fortunes of particular places and people. However, global companies can also stop FDI at short notice. For example, they can decide to stop manufacturing in one factory and move to a cheaper supplier at any time.

> ### Think Point
> What advantages are there for companies such as Nike in subcontracting the manufacture of its goods, and in not selling direct to the public?

> ### Think Point
> Why have some people campaigned about the working practices of global companies such as Nike?

> ### Action Point
> Write down your answers to the following questions:
> 1. How far do you think globalisation has enabled firms like Nike to exist? Would they have been different in some way without today's transport and communication technologies?
> 2. List five environmental consequences of goods being made in locations different from the place where the goods are sold.
> 3. Using the Internet, find out about campaigns against global companies such as Nike. What have the campaigns been about? You can find some websites to help you at www.heinemann.co.uk/hotlinks. Enter the express code 031XP and click on the links.

> ### Think Point
> If a global company withdraws its Foreign Direct Investment from one particular place, who might be affected?

4.8 Global products, global culture

One of the interesting things about globalisation is the spread of similar products around the world. Today, many global brands such as Coca-Cola, Sony, Reebok and Nokia are world-famous – they have become known and are available to people worldwide.

> **Think Point**
>
> Based on your own experience, list five global brands that seem to appear wherever you go.

Coca-Cola is sometimes described as the world's best-known product. Its global spread is so wide, and the demand for the drink is so high, that it cannot be manufactured in one single place. Canners and bottlers are located worldwide – Coca-Cola is manufactured more locally than its global image might suggest. Such factories receive a liquid concentrate directly from The Coca-Cola Company; they add a sweetener, local water and carbon dioxide to it, and complete the manufacturing process by putting the drink into cans or bottles.

Improvements in technology mean that products such as Coca-Cola can be manufactured in some of the world's poorer countries. 'Just-in-time' production methods and technology and virtually instant electronic communication between a global company's head offices and factories around the world help the company to produce its goods globally while reducing transport and administration costs.

> **Think Point**
>
> What advantages are there for (a) the global company, and (b) local people in producing a global product locally? What are the disadvantages?

'Just in time'

Canning and bottling Coca-Cola so that it reaches the supermarket chains and other retailers exactly when they want it is a complex process. To make sure the process runs smoothly, the canners and bottlers must have supplies of the drink, cans and bottles at exactly the right time. Once canned and bottled, Coca-Cola must then be transported just in time to reach the supermarkets when they need it. This all has to be done with precision timing – the canners and bottlers must avoid having large stockpiles of Coca-Cola waiting to be sold, but they must also ensure that they are not waiting for canning and bottling to take place just when the supermarket wants a delivery. Hot weather can affect the process too, as people tend to drink more Coca-Cola in warmer weather. Everything has to be done just in time!

● **Figure 1** A Coca-Cola bottling/canning factory

'Cocacolonisation'

The development of satellite communications has allowed programmes and television channels to appear simultaneously on the world's television networks. Global events can now be beamed into our living rooms as they happen. News that would previously have taken many days (or longer) to spread around the world is communicated as it happens.

Some geographers are concerned that the globalisation of communication may mean that places become increasingly similar. Since wealthier countries – also known as the **developed countries** or the West – dominate the content of the global media, they worry that people in developing countries will follow Western habits and culture such as dress and language at the expense of local habits and culture. Some geographers are unhappy about the global media promoting a particular way of life and describe the spread of Western or American values as 'Cocacolonisation'.

Other geographers, however, argue that places are constantly changing despite globalisation. Although globalisation is increasingly felt in many poorer countries as they become more connected to other countries, these geographers believe that places cannot be frozen in time – they will inevitably change.

Think Point

What does the term 'Cocacolonisation' suggest? Why do you think the term has come about? Think about how far the American media may have influenced the way of life in the UK.

Action Point

1. In recent years, there have been campaigns in Britain to promote locally grown food. Do you think people should 'buy local' or 'buy global', or does it make no difference? Write down your views.
2. Imagine that you are the managing director of a global company that manufactures, advertises and sells a globally known product. How would you use globalisation to maximise your profits?
3. Investigate the idea of 'Cocacolonisation'. Is it a good or a bad thing? Write down your views, giving both sides of the argument.

Assessment

1. Design and carry out an investigation into whether a place in your local area is a 'clone town'. Look back at section 4.5 for information about clone towns. Remember to structure your work clearly, and to explain your findings carefully. Present a professional report to your geography teacher.

2. Visit the website of Llanboidy Cheesemakers, a small Welsh company. Go to www.heinemann.co.uk/hotlinks, enter the express code 031XP and click on the link. The company exports a *local* product to other countries because of its link to the *global* world wide web (the Internet).

   a Explain how improvements in transport and communications have allowed businesses like this to become more global.
   b What use does Llanboidy Cheesemakers' website make of local imagery? Why do you think this is?

3. Using an atlas, plot the places mentioned in the two 'top ten' lists of clone towns on a blank map of the UK. What patterns can you identify?

Top 10 clone towns with least local identity	Top 10 home towns with most local identity
1. Exeter	1. Hebden Bridge
2. Dumfries	2. Peebles
3. Stafford	3. Bo'ness
4. Middlesborough	4. Normanton, West Yorkshire
5. Weston-super-Mare	5. Frodsham
6. Winchester	6. Emsworth
7. Newport	7. Hadleigh, Suffolk
8. Dorchester, Dorset	8. Great Malvern
9. Cheltenham	9. Lewes
10. Burton-on-Trent	10. Gainsborough

Chapter 5

Cybergeography

- **5.1** What is cybergeography?
- **5.2** What is cyberspace?
- **5.3** A space of flows
- **5.4** Changing the 'real' world
- **5.5** Singapore, a wired city
- **5.6** Mapping cyberspace
- **5.7** Holes in cyberspace
- **5.8** The death of real places

5.1 What is cybergeography?

'A science fiction writer coined the term 'cyberspace' in 1982. But the territory in question, the electronic frontier, is about 130 years old. Cyberspace is the 'place' where a telephone conversation appears to occur. Not inside your actual phone, the plastic device on your desk. Not inside the other person's phone, in some other city. *The place between* the phones. The indefinite place *out there*, where the two of you, two human beings, actually meet and communicate.

Although it is not exactly 'real', 'cyberspace' is a genuine place. Things happen there that have very genuine consequences.'

Source: world wide web.

As geographers, we need to be aware that the world is an ever-changing place. You probably know that the new information and communication technologies (ICT), such as the Internet, mobile phones and satellite television, lie behind much change in the world. ICTs change the everyday lives of people, including the businesses in which they work, how they work and the ways in which they communicate with other people – which means that ICTs are also changing today's geography. Such changes are particularly felt in wealthier or Western countries, such as the UK, and in those countries that are **developing** or industrialising, such as India. (Look back at section 4.3, page 54–5, to find out how the new technologies have changed the way businesses and people work.)

Cyberspace refers to the joining together of ICTs, such as telephones or satellite television, to form networks – rather like roads making up a transport network. The difference is that cyberspace is, mostly, an 'invisible' network – we can think of it as a 'virtual' world but one in which people 'meet' and communicate.

Almost everything in our lives has a geography – for example where supermarkets are located, or where our local water supply comes from. Equally, cyberspace has a geography – for example ICT networks are spread out over space, but some places have little or no connection with cyberspace. As geographers, we use the term 'cybergeography' to refer to the geography of cyberspace. It is an increasingly important part of geography, because ICTs are playing an ever-growing part in our lives.

● **Figure 1** Cyberspace – an invisible, worldwide communications network

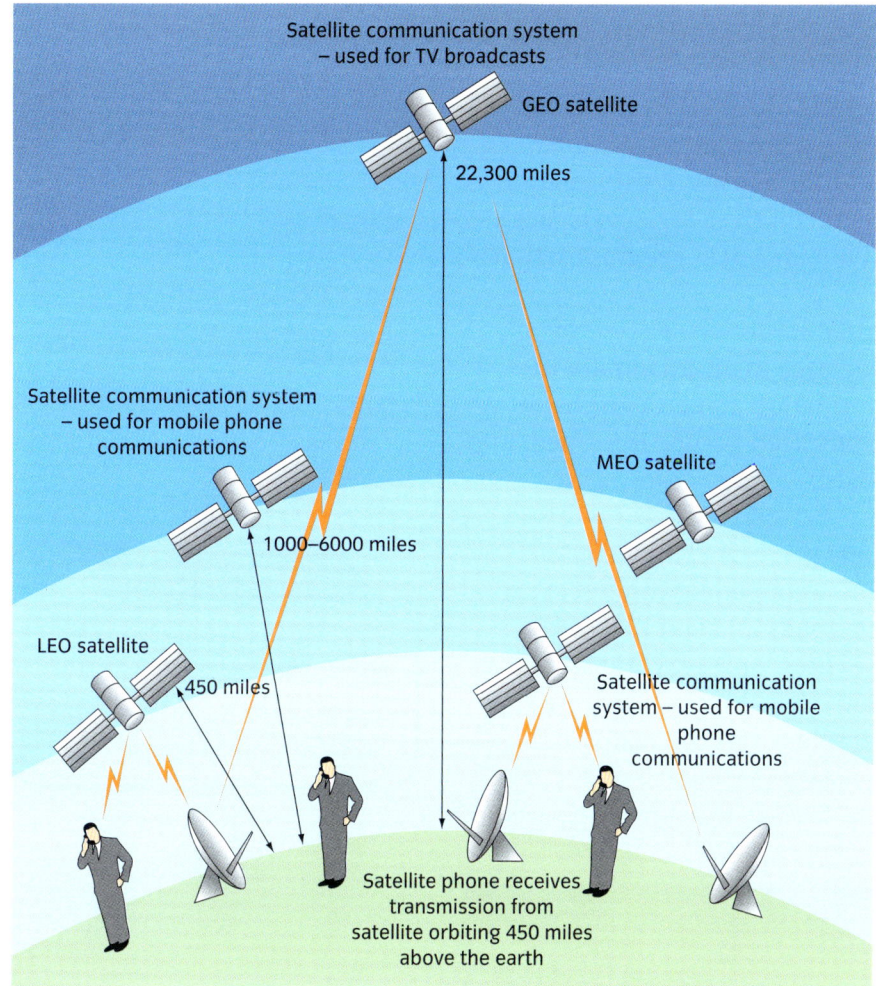

● **Figure 2** Satellite systems orbiting above the earth connect communications networks across the planet

Think Point

What do you think the term 'virtual world' means? Compare your definition with others in your class. Do you all agree?

If we use the term 'cyberspace' for the virtual world, what do you think 'meatspace' might mean?

In this chapter, you will learn about:
- the geography of the 'hardware' of ICTs (such as computers and mobile telephones) and the links between them (such as fibre-optic cables) – in other words, the infrastructure of cyberspace
- the way in which ICTs change the 'real' world, including our everyday lives and the environment in which we live
- whether new kinds of 'places' are created when people communicate online using ICTs, for example when using chatrooms and instant messaging services such as MSN.

Action Point

Investigate the ICTs you have in your home, or at school. Include access to the Internet, telephones (both landline and mobile) and television. Try to make your investigation as detailed as possible, for example you could describe the type of links (satellite; cable; wireless; broadband) you have at home, or at school, and the 'hardware' (such as a specific computer) they connect to. Describe also what access you have to ICTs other than those at home or at school. How 'connected' are you?

5.2 What is cyberspace?

Cyberspace is made up of the networks of the world's information and communications technologies (ICT) hardware – computer networks and mobile telephones – and the **flows** of information within those networks. The networks themselves are cyberspace's physical structure, part of which has a 'hard', real geography that we can plot on maps.

Many geographers also think of cyberspace as an imaginary or invisible world, a place in which information travels worldwide at great speeds, the latest communications keep people informed, and where people can 'chat' to their friends.

Cyberspace is, in some ways, like a real place. It can be explored, for example by surfing the world wide web; people can 'meet' there, for example in chatrooms; and goods and services can be bought and sold. Chatrooms and the 'sites' on the world wide web are not real places, of course, but they may seem real because they offer similar opportunities to those that exist in the real world.

To understand cyberspace, we need to look at the different parts of today's ICT.

Think Point

What does the term 'cybercafé' mean? Is it a real place?

What does the use of the words 'café' and 'cyber' suggest?

● **Figure 1** A cybercafé

The Internet

The Internet is a worldwide network of computers, which is 'wired' together through billions of connections. Each connected computer is part of a network. The computers you use at home or at school are likely to be part of this worldwide network. The technology of the Internet means that the different networks are able to 'talk' to each other, which makes the Internet a huge resource that enables computers (and people) all over the world to communicate with each other. It is a key part of the global 'information superhighway'.

Think Point

What does the term 'information superhighway' suggest?

Email

Email, sent via the Internet, is the most popular online activity – around 31 billion emails are sent every day. Emails can be thought of as electronic versions of traditional letters because, like letters, they are written communications between people. However, they offer advantages over traditional mail – emails can be sent and received almost instantaneously; files of various types and sizes can be attached to them; and they can be sent to large numbers of people at the same time.

The world wide web

The world wide web (www) enables individual computers to communicate with each other via the Internet. Programmes such as Internet Explorer and Netscape allow users to 'surf' websites – in other words, the world wide web allows individual users to connect to another computer regardless of its location, and to explore the information it holds.

One use of the world wide web is online retailing, which is a fast-growing part of the UK economy. This enables people to buy and sell goods and services through cyberspace, rather than face to face in a shop. Such is the popularity of the world wide web that its use is growing rapidly (see table).

● **Figure 2** Number of Internet users worldwide, 1995–2005

Year	Number of users (millions)	Percentage of world population
1995	16	0.4
1997	70	0.9
1999	248	3.6
2001	513	7.9
2003	719	11.1
2005	888	13.9

> **Think Point**
>
> What different types of media can you get access to through the world wide web? Is the world wide web simply a written form of communication? How do organisations like the BBC use their websites?

Internet chatrooms

The Internet enables people to chat worldwide. For example, MSN and Yahoo Chat allow two or more people to communicate directly, either through text, voice or video. Online chat is an alternative both to face-to-face and telephone communication between people: people 'meet' in cyberspace — in the virtual rather than the 'real' world.

Virtual reality

Virtual reality (VR) allows users to enter computer-generated, virtual worlds, either by wearing headsets or by watching a screen. This is a form of cyberspace because users enter an 'unreal' or manufactured world. Common applications are flight simulators for the training of aircraft pilots, and computer games.

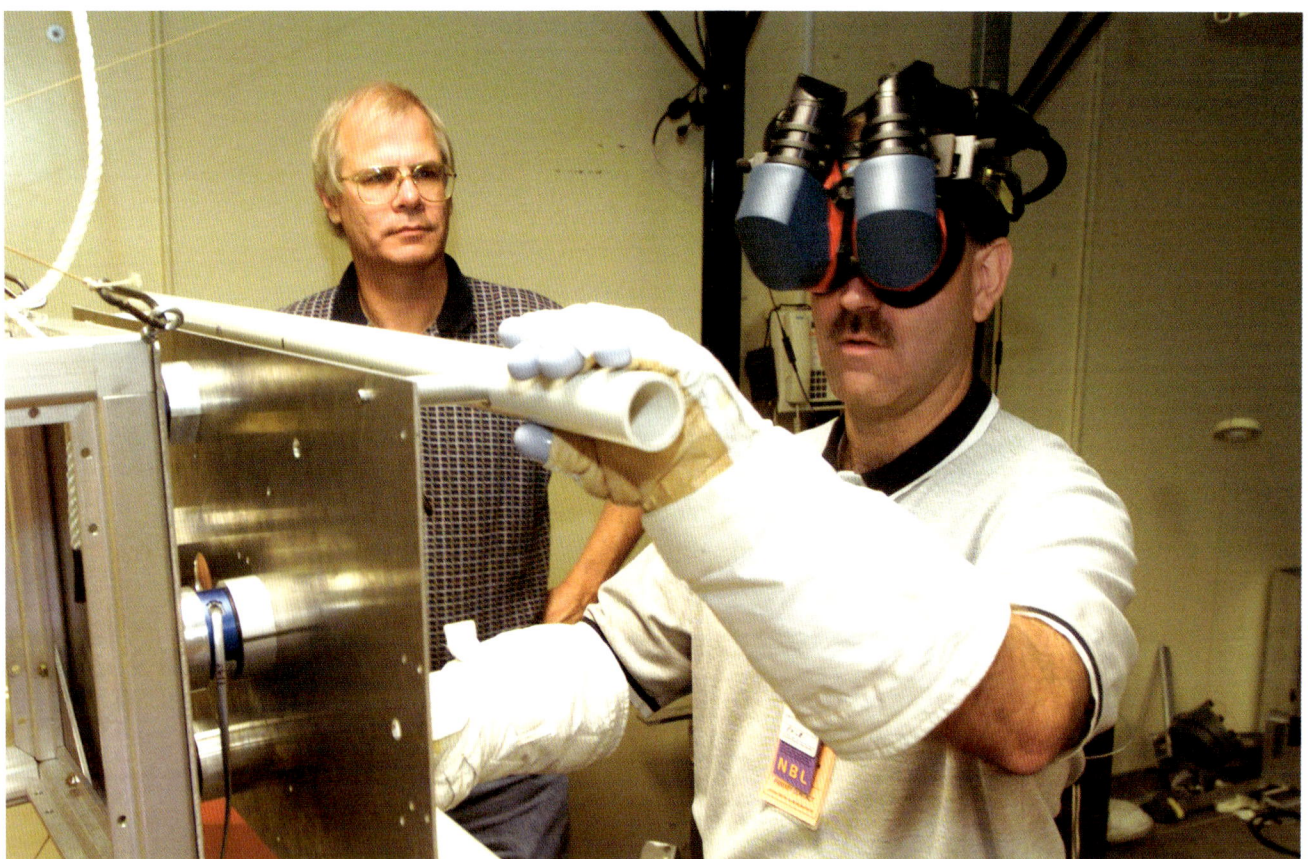

● **Figure 3** Virtual reality: an astronaut training for space travel

Global telephone network

Our world is now linked by an invisible global telephone network. Satellite and cellular technologies allow people to communicate from just about anywhere on the planet, changing the geography and the speed of global communications. Not only is the need for face-to-face meeting unnecessary, new technology means that 'anytime, anyplace' communication is possible for increasing numbers of people across the world.

Action Point

1. Write about your own connection with, and experience, of cyberspace. Include information on which of the technologies you use the most, and explain why. What would your life be like without ICTs?
2. Explain how virtual reality (VR) is different from other forms of cyberspace.

5.3 A space of flows

In Chapter 4, we learned that geography in the twenty-first century is not only concerned with places themselves but also with the flows between those places. In the real world, some of the flows between places may be clearly visible, such as goods being transported on the road by lorry, commuters travelling on the railway to and from towns and cities, and the post being delivered.

The invisible flows that take place within cyberspace are also vitally important to people and businesses. Some of the flows through cyberspace are financially valuable, such as large sums of money being transferred between bank accounts. Others bring important information, such as news of dangerous situations being communicated via satellite television. Still others may be important to individual people, such as an order for goods placed online, or an email bringing news of friends in distant places.

Think Point

Do you think that flows in 'real' space are more important than those in cyberspace? What examples can you think of for visible and 'virtual' flows?

Think about your own daily life – you may chat to your friends online, send and receive emails, and search for information on the Internet, perhaps for your homework. Each time, you are producing some of the many billions of daily flows through cyberspace.

● **Figure 1** The flows of information in cyberspace require physical infrastructure

Action Point

Complete the table below with some examples. Use your own experience where you can. The first example has been filled in for you.

ICT	Type of flow (what did you send or receive?)	Example
Email	Text with an Microsoft Word attachment	An email to a schoolfriend
World wide web		
Instant chat		
Mobile telephone		
		An order for a book
	A sound file (such as an mp3)	
	A text (SMS) message	

Learning Point

Before we continue, let's check that you understand:
- what cyberspace is
- your own experience of cyberspace
- why cyberspace is important to people
- why cyberspace is a place of flows.

Chapter 5 Cybergeography

5.4 Changing the 'real' world

Although cyberspace may not be immediately obvious in the built environment (the 'real' world), information and communication technologies (ICT) are having a real effect on the geography of everyday life, as the examples below illustrate.

The increasing speed and geographical coverage of ICT has enabled businesses to change the way in which they work. For example, global companies such as the car maker Ford and the food manufacturer Nestlé can spread out their operations on a global scale because it is as easy to communicate globally as it is within a single site. Such companies can now take advantage of geographical differences in the world so that goods may be produced in low-cost locations, such as India, while the company's headquarters are in another part of the world, such as the USA.

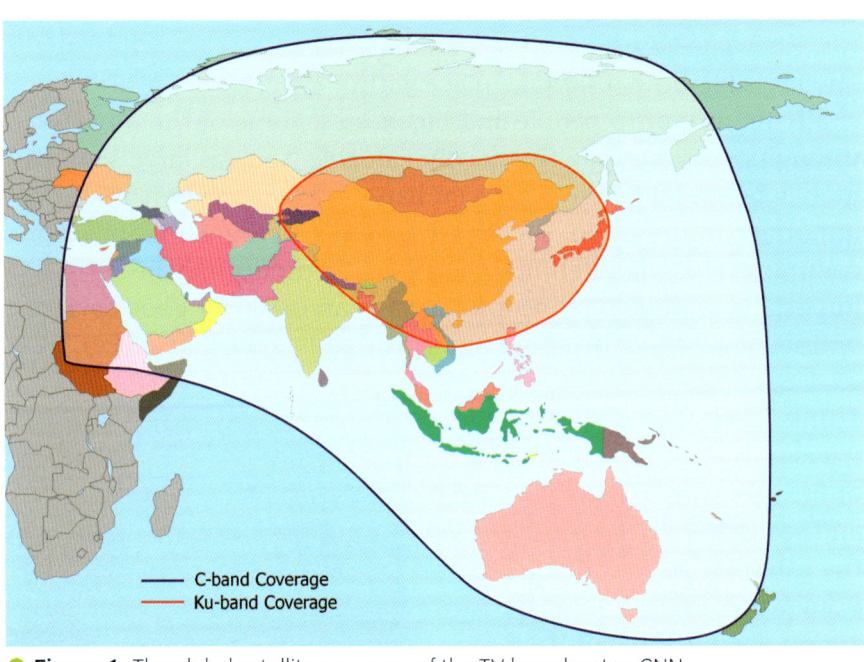

● **Figure 1** The global satellite coverage of the TV broadcaster, CNN

Some geographers argue that the spread of the Internet and satellite television has led to the spread of western (and specifically US) culture and values to other parts of the world:

> '... television around the world is becoming ever more saturated with American shows, Hollywood dominates cinema, radios play music by American artists to people wearing American-branded clothing eating in American fast-food restaurants. In terms of the Internet, the largest and most popular websites are those owned and operated in the US. The majority of the world's computers also run operating systems on application software created by US corporations.'

Source: Martin Dodge and Rob Kitchen.

In the past, people could communicate either face-to-face, over a fixed telephone line where it was installed, or where they were able to receive post. Today's ICTs mean that people have a far greater amount of geographical freedom – they can be connected to cyberspace and the information superhighway without having to remain in one place. For example, tourists travelling around the world can use Internet cafés to keep in touch with people at home.

Think Point

To what extent does quick and easy global communication mean that the distance between places is less important?

Think Point

Is 'any time, any place' communication a good thing? Are there any disadvantages?

The combination of the world wide web, email and modern telephone networks has led to changes in the way people work. Before the 1990s, people tended to travel to work at specific locations and to work fairly fixed hours. Transport developments during the nineteenth century meant that homes and workplaces could be separated geographically. Today's 'information society' means that, for some people, this trend can be reversed. Some people can work as effectively from home (or even cars and trains via wireless technology) than they can from a fixed workplace. This idea of teleworking – working from flexible locations – has the benefit of reducing travelling time and air pollution, and can save businesses money by reducing the need for office space.

> **Action Point**
>
> Find out about the practice of 'hotdesking' in offices. How far do you think it has been enabled by ICT?

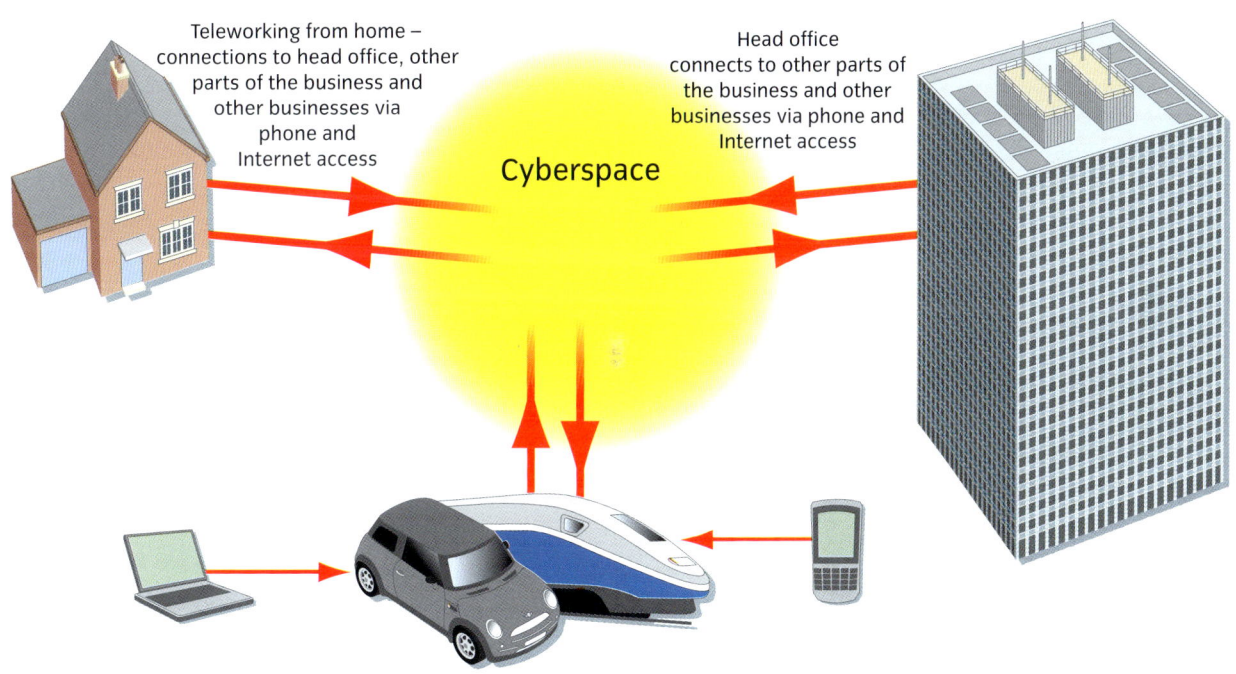

● **Figure 2** Teleworking

People's quality of life can be affected by the extent to which the places in which they live and work are connected to the information superhighway. Economic geographers have noted that the countries with the most successful economies are those where there are high levels of access to ICT, for example Singapore has placed cyberspace at the heart of its economy and of everyday life.

Individual people who have access to cyberspace are advantaged – they have access to more information, they have the opportunity to communicate more easily and quickly, and they can take advantage of the social connections offered by ICT. On a large scale, cyberspace offers individuals many opportunities to broaden their life chances compared to people without ICT connections. Cyberspace can also help people with mobility problems with everyday tasks like shopping and communication.

> **Action Point**
>
> 1. To what extent is your life, and that of your family, influenced by your connections to cyberspace? Write down some examples of how cyberspace has, or might be able to, change your daily routine.
> 2. Why are people who are connected to the information superhighway considered to be advantaged? How far do you agree with this? Write a brief argument.

5.5 Singapore: a wired city

The economic growth of Singapore has been spectacular. In the 1960s, its gross domestic product per head, which is the average of each person's output, was a fairly low US$1300; by the early twenty-first century, it was US$38,000. Singapore has transformed itself from one of the world's poorer cities to one of its wealthier ones, and from an economy with a large, unskilled labour force producing many items in factories to an economy with a much smaller, highly skilled workforce producing sophisticated electronic items, such as microchips.

● Figure 1 Singapore

What has caused such remarkable success? Much of the answer lies in information and communication technologies (ICT), and the Singapore government's determination to make Singapore one of the world's first 'wired' or 'soft' cities – where as many people and businesses as possible have easy, fast and cheap access to cyberspace, and the city is linked by fast Internet connections and high levels of mobile telephone ownership and coverage.

To this end, in 1992, the Singapore government announced a policy – known as IT2000 – to put together a team of experts to oversee the building of a 'National Information Infrastructure', which would:

- create a highly skilled, ICT workforce
- improve people's quality of life through ICT
- give Singapore an economic advantage over other countries by investing heavily in ICTs and connections to cyberspace.

● Figure 2 Singapore in south-east Asia

'In our vision, some fifteen years from now, Singapore, the Intelligent Island, will be among the first countries in the world with an advanced nation-wide infrastructure. It will interconnect computers in virtually every home, office, school and factory. The computer will evolve into an information appliance, combining the functions of the telephone, computer, TV and more. It will provide a wide range of communication modes and access to services. Text, sound, pictures, video, documents, designs and other forms of media can be transferred and shared through this broadband information infrastructure made up of fibre-optic cables reaching to all homes and offices, and a wireless network working in tandem. The information infrastructure will also permeate our physical infrastructure making mobile tele-computing possible, and our homes, work places, airport, seaport and surface transportation systems "smarter".'

Source: Singapore National Computer Board, IT2000: *A Vision of an Intelligent Island*, 1991.

Singapore planned at a very early stage to use high-quality ICT networks, combined with an expert workforce, to transform its economy and improve its citizens' lives. The ICT network enabled Singapore's businesses to communicate quickly and easily with their customers and other businesses inside and outside Singapore, largely before other countries saw the need to do so. This enabled the city to become a developer and an exporter of ICT expertise, and in this way it was able to join the small group of the world's wealthy, technologically advanced economies.

Singapore's IT2000 policy has now given way to Infocomm21, a new policy that aims to transform Singapore into a 'vibrant ICT capital' by 2010. Singapore has welcomed the 'information society' revolution, and has encouraged the growth of dot.com businesses. Singapore's success has been so great that in 2005 it overtook the United States to secure first place in a league table of countries making the best use of ICT.

Think Point

What is your opinion of Singapore's IT2000 policy? Given that the policy was successful, how different is Singapore in terms of ICTs from the place in which you live?

Action Point

Write your answers to the following questions:
1. What advantages do you think early planning brought to Singapore? Were they sufficient on their own to bring about economic success?
2. Find out if any other places have attempted to become 'wired' cities? Carry out an Internet search to provide evidence to support your answer.

Learning Point

Before we continue, let's check that you understand:
- how cyberspace changes the 'real' world
- why becoming 'wired' may benefit places economically.

5.6 Mapping cyberspace

Maps are central to the study of geography – we cannot study places effectively without them. Although cyberspace is often thought of as an imaginary or 'unreal' place, geographers are becoming increasingly interested in mapping cyberspace.

Maps of cyberspace come in various forms. Some are based on geographic space, some are based on ideas, while others attempt to represent cyberspace artistically. This fascinating aspect of cybergeography brings together one of the oldest aspects of geography – map making – with one of its most recent. This section illustrates just four cybermaps to show the wide variety available.

Figure 1 is a very early cybermap, and represents the flows of Internet traffic in the United States in November 1993.

Think Point
Why might geographers wish to map cyberspace?

Think Point
What do you think the cybermap in Figure 1 would look like today?

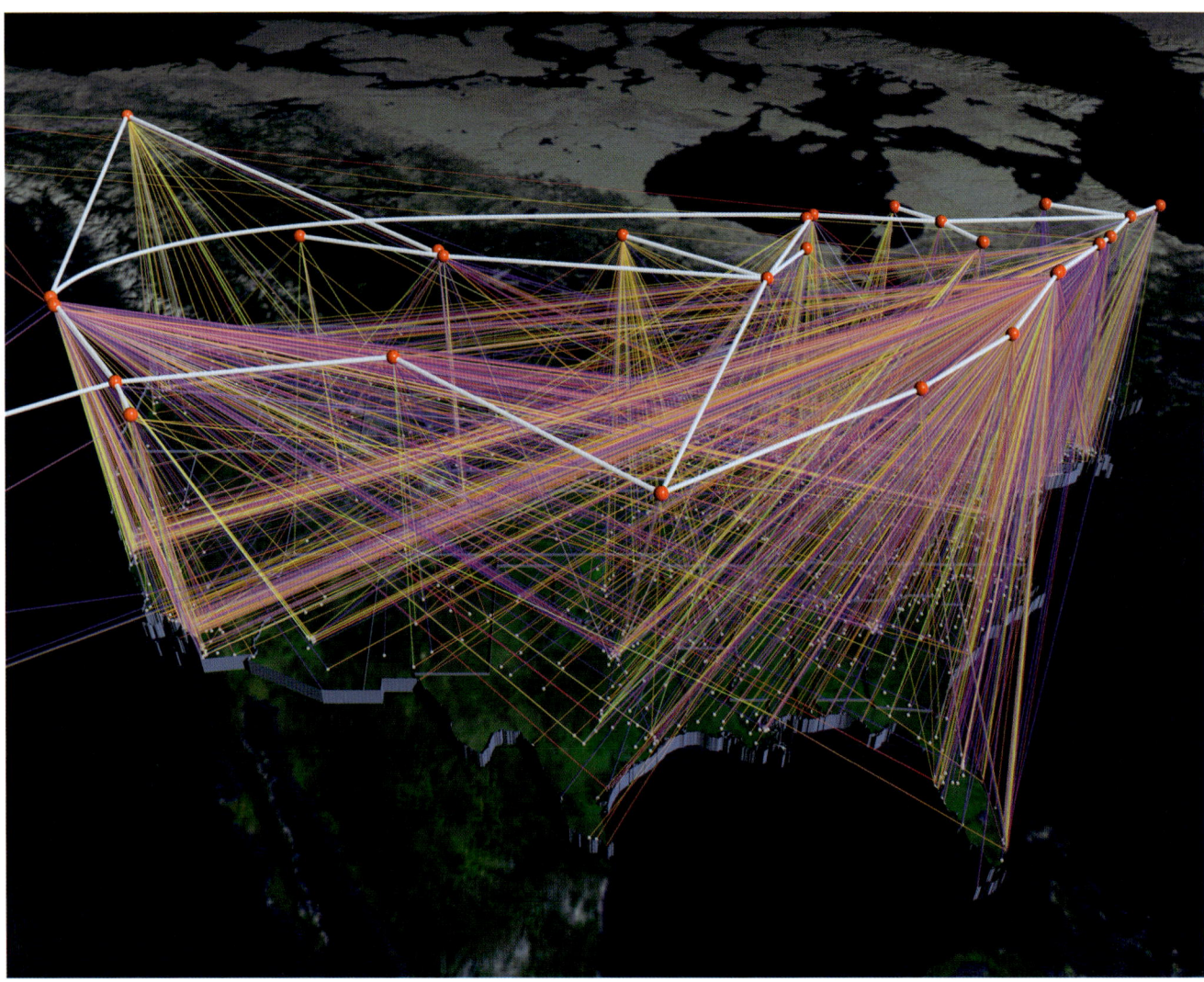

● **Figure 1** An early cybermap of Internet traffic in the United States

Figure 2 shows mobile telephone connections in central London. The green circles and triangles represent transmitters.

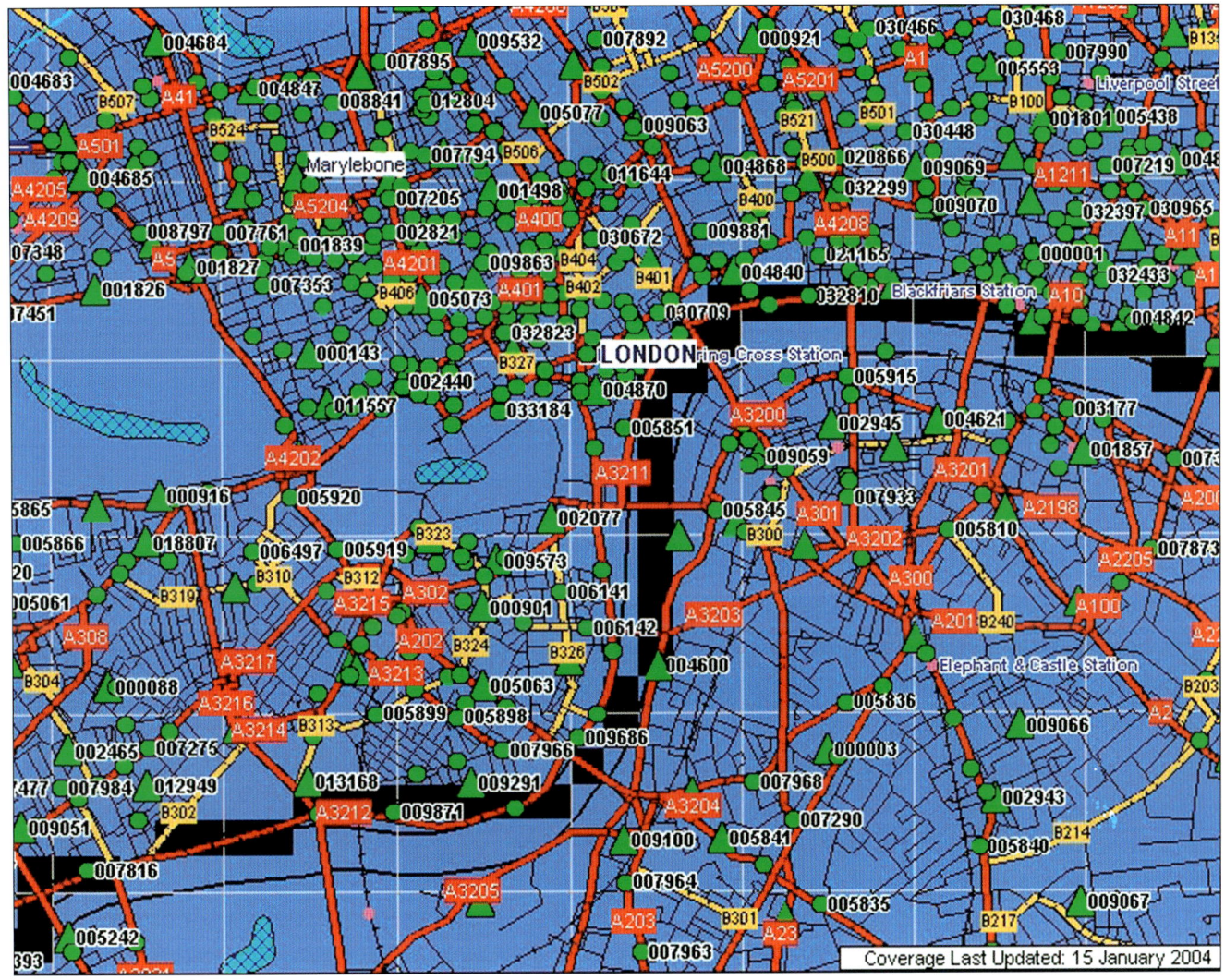

- **Figure 2** Mobile telephone connections in central London

Think Point

Look at Figure 2. How far do you think people in London are aware of the cyberspace infrastructure that surrounds them?

Figure 3 is a computer-generated image of cyberspace, reflecting its physical dimension as well as the time taken for information to travel. RTT stands for Round-trip Time – the time taken for an item of data to be sent in cyberspace, and a response received from its destination.

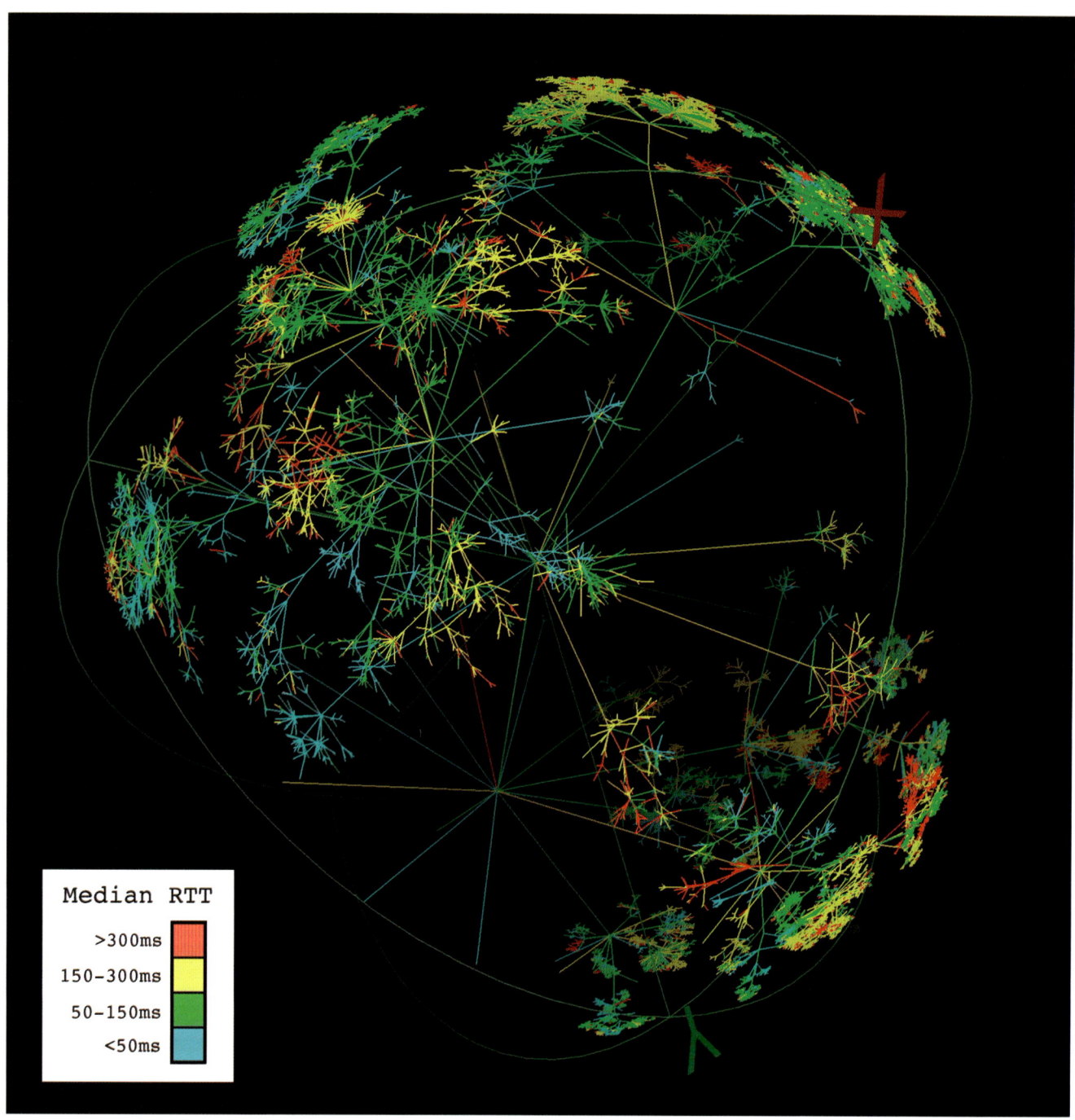

● **Figure 3** A computer-generated image of cyberspace

Think Point

Look for Europe in Figure 3. Can you see any other places? Where are connections slowest?

Figure 4 shows the network of Interoute, one of Europe's network providers – it enables massive volumes of data to flow through cyberspace.

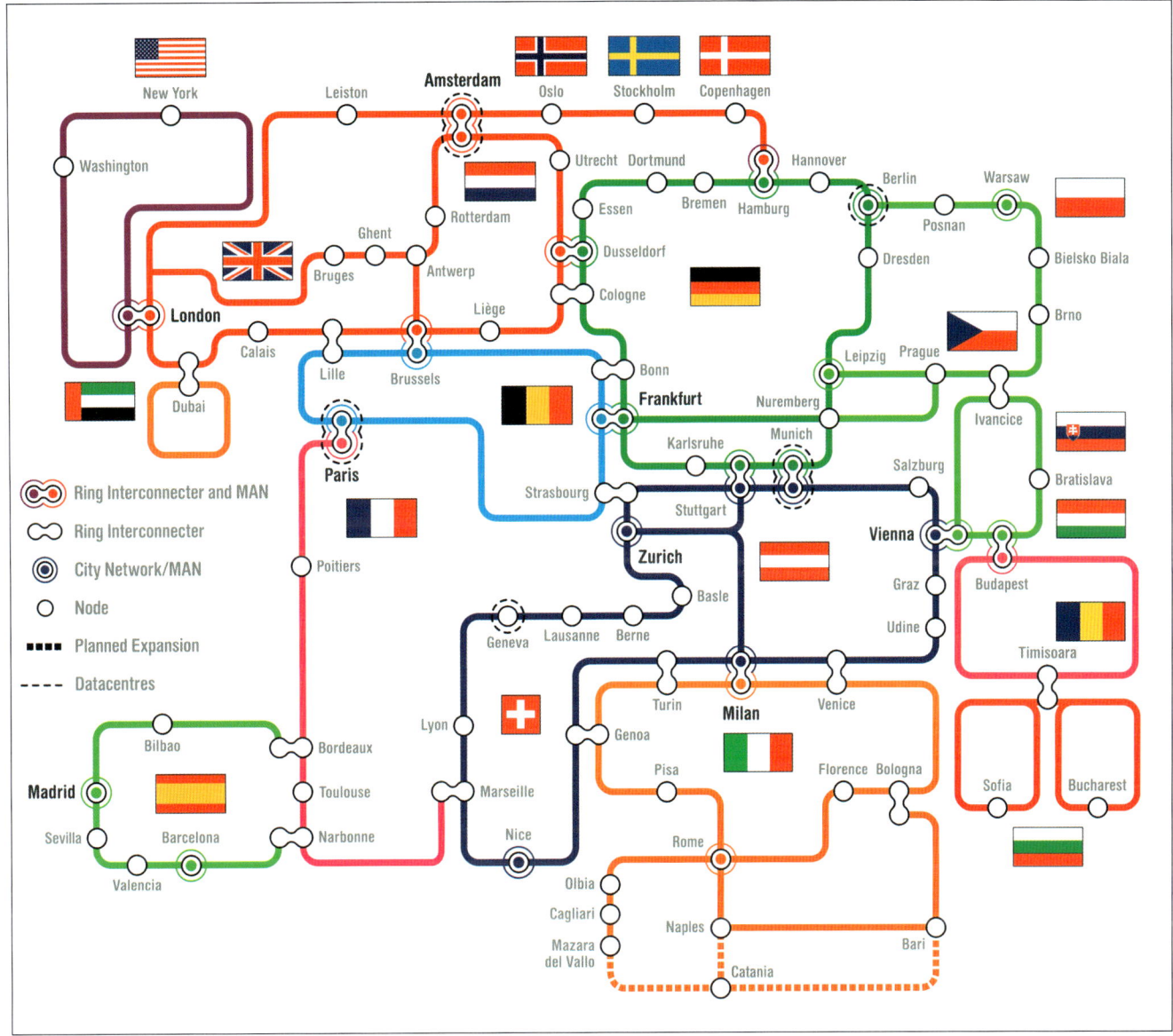

- Figure 4 A cybermap of Interoute, an ICT network provider

Think Point

Why do you think the cybermap in Figure 4 is presented in this way?

Action Point

1. If you can (you will need permission), use the Internet Cartographer 2.0 programme to visualise web surfing at home or at school. How useful is it? What does it tell you about the geography of your personal Internet usage?
2. Explore the Cyber Geography website. Include the artistic maps in your surfing. How many different types of cybermap can you identify? Which are the most useful? And the most visually attractive?
3. Use the O2 online mapping service to plot the mobile telephone infrastructure in your area and the network coverage. How does your area compare with others? Go to www.heinemann.co.uk/hotlinks and enter the express code 031XP to find links to both of these websites.

5.7 Holes in cyberspace

The information superhighway brings many benefits for businesses and people. For example, being 'connected' means that businesses can sell to more customers globally, and people can keep in touch cheaply and easily. Information and communications technology (ICT) connections have the power to improve people's quality of life.

A key aspect of cybergeography is the uneven access to cyberspace across the world. The information superhighway is at its most developed in richer, **western countries**, such as the UK, but the world's poorest countries, particularly in some parts of Asia and Africa, have limited, if any, access. Geographers call this difference the 'digital divide'.

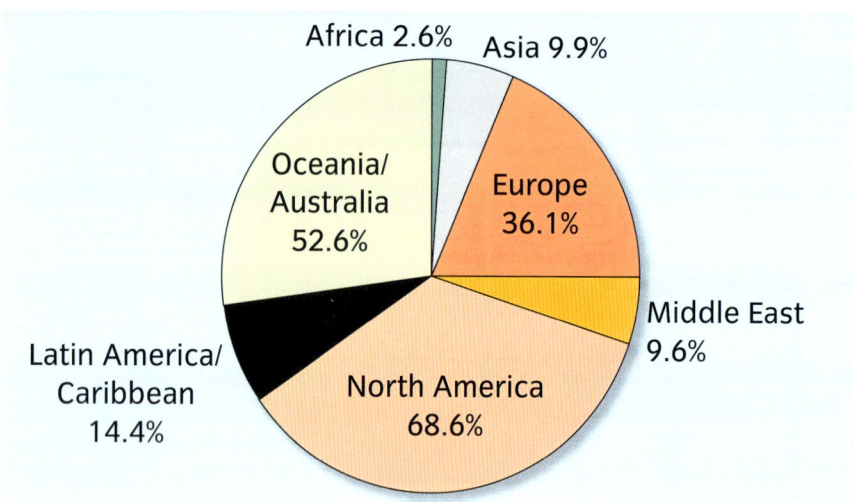

● **Figure 1** Percentage of population with access to the Internet, by world region, 2006
Source: the Internet World Statistics website

There are many factors that cause this unevenness, including the lack of network **infrastructure** in poorer countries, and the high cost of access compared to people's earnings. In some countries, such as China, the government restricts access to the Internet – some websites cannot be viewed.

In geography, we study phenomena at a range of different scales – local, national, and global, for example. The 'digital divide' is no exception. It can be seen at a local level, for example on the border between cities and the countryside; at a national level; and at international and global scales. Places can be divided into information superhighway 'haves' and 'have-nots', as shown in the table opposite.

Think Point

Why is the information superhighway mainly available only in richer countries?

Do you think it should expand geographically?

Think Point

What initiatives could be put in place to help the world's least developed countries gain access to the Internet?

Figure 2 The digital divide in the UK

wealthier people		poorer people
town dwellers	are more likely to have computers and Internet connections than:	rural folk
able-bodied people		people with disabilities
white people		ethnic minorities
younger people		older people

Source: the Flexibility website

> **Think Point**
>
> How did Singapore avoid the problem of the digital divide? Look back at section 5.5.

Those who are unable to access the Internet are excluded from many opportunities in society, such as the use of the world wide web for information-seeking (or shopping), and the ability to communicate with people quickly and easily though email. In rural areas, the Internet offers people social opportunities, for example through email and in chatrooms. These opportunities could never exist in 'real' space because of the small numbers of people spread over a large geographical area. People in places with low population density, provided they have a telephone line, computer and modem, can connect in cyberspace much more quickly and easily than in the 'real' world.

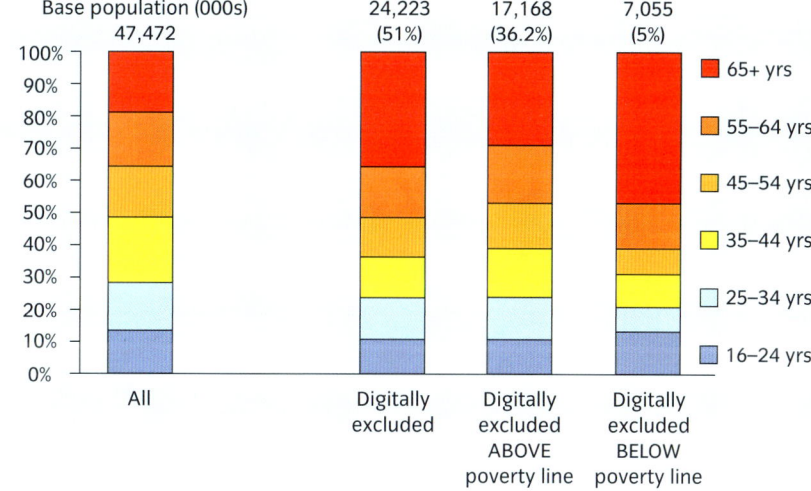

Figure 3 People with no access to the information superhighway (digitally excluded) in the UK, 2004

> **Think Point**
>
> Imagine you are someone on the 'unconnected' side of the digital divide. Would it matter to you if you had no Internet access? Or a mobile phone?

The digital divide creates a new geography of exclusion at local, regional, national and global scales. The Internet, and the information that flows though its cyberspace, has the power to transform the financial opportunities of people and places, as we saw in section 5.5 on Singapore.

Even so, only 50 per cent of the world's population has access to a telephone line, and 77 per cent to a mobile phone network. It is important to remember that although people may technically have access to cyberspace, in many poorer countries the cost of access may be unaffordable for large parts of the population.

5.8 The death of real places

Do we need real places any more? Throughout this chapter, we have seen that it is possible for people – particularly those in wealthier countries – to carry out many parts of their daily lives through cyberspace. For example, we can communicate with people by email, telephone, videoconferencing and online chat; we can buy almost anything online, and have it delivered to our home; we can keep up to date with the latest news from around the world through satellite or cable links; and many people can now work, and learn, at home.

> **Think Point**
>
> Between April 2000 and December 2005, online shopping in the UK grew by 2600 per cent, from £87 million to £2.26 billion. What are the most likely consequences of this change for people and places?

Each of these examples means that people might choose to leave their homes less frequently. It could be argued, perhaps, that cyberspace means that many of us need not leave our homes at all! In turn, this could mean that 'real' shops, schools, universities, and cafés, might become increasingly redundant in favour of 'virtual' replacements. Now, read about the Dumill family in 2020.

The Dumill family, Pluckley, Kent, 2025

Mr Dumill was sitting in his study, working on his next broadcast to his students, and listening to his favourite French radio station. Since the school had closed in 2015, he had quickly grown accustomed to working at home. He didn't miss the 45-minute daily commute through the Channel Tunnel to the lycée in Calais. No more school run either for Timberlake (14) or Jordan (11): their own e-learning broadcasts would download to the digital wall in their study-bedrooms at 0900, automatically closing down chat programmes and Internet access – apart from when they were required for learning, of course.

In the kitchen, Mrs Dumill was happily surfing the Internet on the family's new digital plasma-fridge combo, searching for online airline bargains. The money the family saved each year on petrol always disappeared quickly on an extra family holiday to the Ukrainian eco-lodge they had bought.

(Continued on p.85)

At 0930 the Chinese-made fridge let out a short series of beeps, and Mrs Dumill went to the front door. As usual, the fridge's GPS alert was precisely accurate: the green hydrogen-powered Waitsco van was pulling up outside with the weekly shopping, all of the food organic, and most of it locally produced. Mrs Dumill smiled as she recalled the hours she used to spend in the supermarket. Things were so much easier now the fridge was wirelessly networked with the kitchen cupboards, and the e-fridge could order the family's needs after comparing prices between the online supermarkets. She pressed the green button on the driver's e-pod, instantly sending €300 from her bank account to Waitsco's.

The lights flickered momentarily – they did around this time every day – as the domestic management system switched over to solar power. The daily email from Czechelec arrived on Mr Dumill's e-pod: to tell them how much they had earned yesterday by selling electricity to the Eurasian grid. Just enough to download a vintage *Coronation Street* from 2006, he thought as he began his broadcast; it was good to be reminded of real people in real places, and the old days.

With apologies to Professor Peter Hall, who first created the Dumill family

Action Point

1. How realistic do you think the 2020 scenario of the Dumills' household might be? Suggest reasons for your answer.
2. In the Dumills' household, the fictitious e-pod was used twice. If you had to design an item of technology that linked with cyberspace, and changed people's daily lives, what would it be like? Write a detailed explanation.
3. If more and more of people's everyday lives can take place through cyberspace, what might this mean for real places? Write about this in around 250 words.
4. Write a detailed assessment of how much of your 'real world' activities could take place through cyberspace. What would be the consequences for you personally if you switched those activities to cyberspace? What might be the effects on the places you no longer visited?

The growth in the use of cyberspace may well enable people to travel less, so bringing about some environmental benefits, and for people whose movement from home is restricted, a connection with cyberspace might improve their quality of life.

Think Point

How might people who are less mobile benefit from technologies such as the Internet?

Learning Point

Before we continue, let's check that you understand:
- how cyberspace can be mapped
- why being on the 'wrong' side of the digital divide may exclude people from a variety of opportunities
- why some geographers suggest that 'real' places may be less important in the future
- whether your own experience (or lack of it) with cyberspace changes your everyday life.

Assessment

As geographers, one of the most important skills that we need to have is the ability to speculate about how places may change in the future. The best geographers are able to look forward in the same way as historians look backward. In this assessment, you will be asked to build on the scenario of the Dumills' household in 2020 (see section 5.8).

Having considered a number of aspects of cybergeography, it seems clear that:

- cyberspace and information and communication technologies (ICT) will change over time
- cyberspace will increasingly change people's everyday lives
- cybergeography will change over time (as ICTs evolve) and space (different places will be affected by cyberspace in different ways).

Now, produce your own piece of creative writing: an imaginary scenario about everyday people and places in 30 years' time. You may wish to consider the following questions before you start to write:

- How might ICT (including virtual reality) change in the future?
- How would you like ICT to change in the future?
- What might cyberspace be like?
- How might different places in the world change?
- How might your everyday life be different?

Remember the importance of the accurate use of English in your answer. Try to structure your work clearly. Include maps and diagrams where appropriate. You may wish, if you have access, to use the world wide web to help your investigation.

Chapter 6

Geographies of consumption

- 6.1 People as consumers
- 6.2 Right or responsibility?
- 6.3 Consumption in the landscape
- 6.4 The production-consumption chain
- 6.5 The effect of our decisions
- 6.6 Who decides?
- 6.7 The coolhunters
- 6.8 Fair trade

6.1 People as consumers

Imagine yourself in a busy town centre watching what the people are doing there. You would probably think that some people are working, others are shopping, socialising or simply passing the time of day. At first glance, it might seem unimportant to know this, but think again! As geographers, we need to be interested in people's everyday lives, because people's daily actions have real consequences for geography itself.

Figure 1 A busy day in Merthyr Tydfil

Let's imagine now that you buy something from the shops – a pair of jeans, for example. On the face of it, this is quite a straightforward transaction – you get the jeans; the retailer gets your money. If we were to investigate a little further, though, we would find that your purchase had many geographical consequences. In order for you to 'consume' (buy and then wear) the jeans, they had first to be produced and then transported. For example, the cotton may have been grown in Pakistan, the denim manufactured in Milan, and the jeans sewn together in a Vietnamese factory using parts (such as zips) from around the world. The finished jeans would then have been transported in several stages to the shop in which you bought them.

In this example, it is likely that your money would be scattered across perhaps 20 different places around the world, and then to many people in each of those places in the form of wages.

Now, imagine yourself back in the busy town centre. Many of the people you see will also be buying goods and services – they will be behaving as **consumers**. They too will be making daily decisions about their **consumption** – deciding what to buy and where to spend their money. In doing so, they – like you – will send money all over the world.

On an even larger scale, we could think about the many millions of transactions that take place in the UK, or Europe, each day. To try to draw a map of the geographical consequences of those decisions by consumers would be a huge task! We can imagine, though, the many millions of **flows** of goods and money between places around the world – they are all the direct consequence of decisions by consumers.

Think Point

If you owned a jeans manufacturing company, to which other companies and people might you need to pay money for production and transport?

Think Point

Why do you think that only a small proportion of the purchase price of goods often reaches the producer?

Action Point

1. Explain the idea of the production-transport-consumption sequence.
2. Do you think that consumers depend on producers, or do producers depend on consumers? Or do you think the relationship between them is more complex? Explain your answer.
3. Often, the place where goods are produced is different from where they are consumed – sometimes production and consumption occurs thousands of miles apart (coffee is just one example). What do you think are the geographical consequences?

6.2 Right or responsibility?

Consumption is a bigger idea than just 'buying things', or 'using things up'! Experiences can be consumed, such as watching television, texting a friend or going to a pop concert. These are all examples of consumption and our actions, as we saw in section 6.1, have direct geographical consequences.

We take decisions about consumption throughout our daily lives. They may be fairly simple ones, such as what to have for lunch, or more time-consuming ones, such as choosing the colour to decorate a room at home, or where to go on holiday. You may have experiences of agonising over which clothes to buy, or which brand of trainers best suits your image (or budget). The important point is that we all act as consumers.

Consumers in wealthier countries often have (and increasingly demand) much choice – think of the variety of goods offered in large supermarkets, or the range of shops in city centres. Consumers often feel that their spending gives them 'rights' – perhaps to a high-quality product, or to good customer service.

Rights, however, bring responsibilities, and consumers in one place can have a major effect on people's lives in other places. The products we decide to buy (or not buy) can affect a variety of people in many different ways. For example, if a British supermarket decides to stop selling a particular brand of coffee because of poor sales, that decision could result in poverty for the plantation workers and owners who produce that coffee several thousand miles away.

What we consume is often produced not just on a local or regional scale but on a global one. People in one part of the world often depend on consumption habits in other parts of the world for their income, and to maintain their standard of living. Usually, it is the poorer countries that rely on consumption of their goods and services in wealthier countries. It is important, therefore, that we recognise that, as consumers, we are powerful people.

> **Think Point**
> Does all consumption require money to change hands?

● **Figure 1** Making consumption decisions

> **Think Point**
> Do you think that all consumption is essential?

> **Think Point**
> List five examples where you have been a consumer. If you (and many other consumers) were to stop buying any of these items, what do you think would be the consequences for those who produce and sell them?

Action Point

1. Make a list of the resources (physical things you have used, or food!), services (such as transport) or experiences (for example watching television) you have consumed today. Try to think of ten different items.
2. Explain how, when we make consumption decisions, people in other parts of the world can be affected. Remember that there may be positive effects as well as negative ones.

6.3 Consumption in the landscape

The importance of consumption to **Western** societies can be seen clearly in the landscape. Factories and offices are needed to produce goods, services and experiences, and there are also places that would not exist without consumption of those goods and services, for example shops, cinemas and leisure centres.

Shopping is one obvious example of consumption, so let's look at the impact that shopping has had on the physical landscape.

Regional shopping centres

Regional shopping centres are purpose-built, usually enclosed, shopping malls in non-central locations. The largest ones contain several hundred retail outlets. They serve large geographical areas, and are accessible both by public transport and by car. They offer similar services to the city centres — shops, banks, parking, public areas, public transport. There are only a few regional shopping centres in the UK, for example Merry Hill in the West Midlands, Bluewater in Kent, and Meadowhall in Sheffield.

> **Think Point**
>
> Read the information about Merry Hill. Why do you think regional shopping centres might appeal to some people, but not to others?

> **Think Point**
>
> Some geographers describe regional shopping centres as 'cathedrals of consumption'. Why do you think this is?

Merry Hill shopping centre

- Merry Hill shopping centre and Waterfront leisure and office complex are located adjacent to Brierley Hill Town Centre in the West Midlands, 12 miles to the west of Birmingham and 5 miles from the M5 motorway.
- Today Merry Hill is one of the region's most successful shopping destinations, attracting over 21 million visits every year.
- Merry Hill includes over 200 stores undercover, an external retail park and over 10,000 parking spaces.
- The centre offers a wealth of high quality services and facilities.
- The Waterfront offers office space, hosting major businesses such as Egg.com, Barclays, Inland Revenue and the Child Support Agency, and bars and restaurants.

Figure 1 Merry Hill regional shopping centre

Source: the Westfield Merry Hill website

Out-of-town shopping centres

Out-of-town shopping centres generally include between ten and 30 large retail outlets, and are an important part of the consumption landscape. Much smaller than regional shopping centres, their retail uses vary, although usually they consist of national or international retailers. On the same site, there could be shops offering DIY goods, sports equipment, clothing, furniture, etc. Fast-food chains often locate in out-of-town shopping centres.

The centres were mainly designed for car users. Their non-central location and design – there are often few footpaths – may exclude non-motorists and people with restricted mobility.

During the 1980s, there was a dramatic increase in the number of out-of-town shopping centres, as well as in much larger regional shopping centres. More recently, though, central government has realised the environmental damage done by significant numbers of unnecessarily lengthy car journeys to such centres, and has restricted further developments.

Figure 2 An out-of-town shopping centre

The corner shop

At the local scale, the corner shop remains an important part of the consumption landscape, providing a service for the people in that community. They are usually owned by small independent retailers who have just one shop, or a small chain, although there are some nationwide brands such as Spar. In urban areas, such shops are coming under increasing pressure from national retailers – think about the growth of garage-based convenience stores, such as Tesco Metro, and smaller supermarkets like Sainsbury's Local.

> **Think Point**
>
> Do you think local shops have social benefits?

● **Figure 3** A traditional corner shop

> **Learning Point**
>
> Before we continue, let's check that you understand:
> - what consumption is (you should be able to give some examples)
> - how consumers' decisions affect a variety of other people, sometimes in other countries
> - the different ways in which we can see consumption in the landscape (you should be able to give some examples from your own area).

> **Action Point**
>
> 1. List the main differences between the various retail landscapes. You could put your answers in a table.
> 2. Write down why you think different types of retail landscape exist.
> 3. Are different types of retail locations better for some people than others? In your answer, think about people with limited mobility, single parents, or those without cars. Might they feel excluded?

6.4 The production-consumption chain

So how is it possible (or sensible) that products we buy locally are produced on the other side of the world? We might think that products and services should be produced reasonably close to where they are consumed, in order to reduce time delays and transport costs.

The answer lies in the production-consumption chain. An example is shown in Figure 1. Products may be grown or manufactured in one part of the world, then exported to another country for processing, with the final product assembled in yet another country, and lastly sold to retailers (such as supermarkets) in other countries, from which consumers buy them. The production-consumption chain gives our everyday consumption decisions a global meaning, and links us either directly or indirectly with people in other countries.

Think Point

Why do you think that production and consumption occur in different places?

Does it matter that sites of production and consumption are sometimes hundreds or thousands of miles apart?

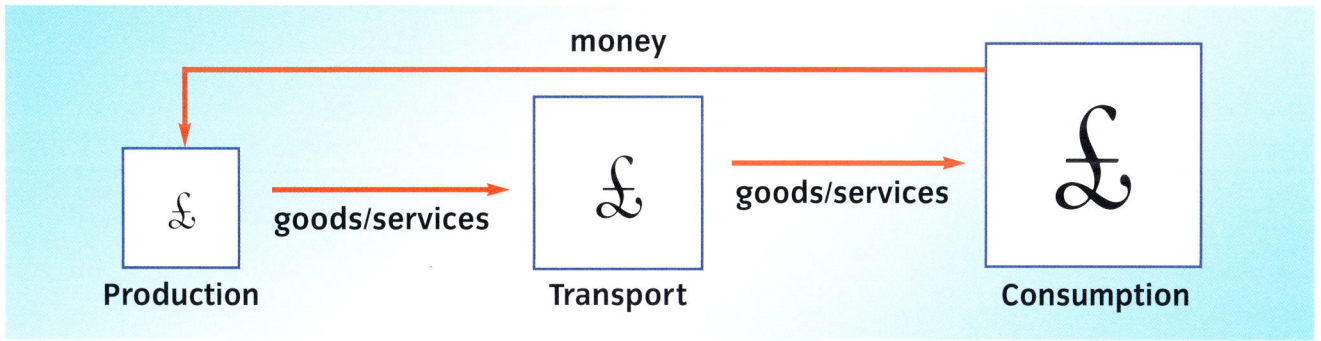

● **Figure 1** A simple production-consumption chain

These links – which geographers describe as '**flows**' – mean that, across the world, countries are dependent upon one another in many different ways. In the UK, for example, we rely on other countries to produce a whole range of everyday items, from potatoes to PlayStations. Equally important, those places that produce the goods rely on the money we pay for their products in order to maintain incomes and employment.

Interdependence is not just limited to goods. It applies to services as well: for example, British companies export engineering and biotechnology expertise to other countries where such knowledge is not available.

Another example of interdependence can be found in the ownership of businesses. One case is in the car manufacturing industry, where workers at the Nissan plant in Sunderland depend on a Japanese company for jobs and therefore their incomes.

Interdependence means that, across the world, there are many **flows** of goods, services and money between the world's producers and consumers (the production-consumption chain). There are so many that they would be impossible to map.

Action Point

'Before you finish eating breakfast this morning, you've depended on more than half the world' (Martin Luther King). Using evidence from home – think about electronic goods, look in your kitchen cupboards, wardrobe, etc. – write about 500 words to explain whether you agree with this comment or not.

6.5 The effect of our decisions

So far, we have discussed the idea that our consumption decisions have consequences for 'other places', the places where the goods and services we consume are produced. Below are three examples of how people, acting as consumers, can cause real changes for people and places.

Workers in tears as NEC shuts factory

Electronics giant NEC has announced the closure of its semi-conductor plant in West Lothian with the loss of more than 1,200 jobs. The company broke the news to employees, blaming a global downturn in demand.

Many were left in tears at the announcement, the latest blow to Scotland's once buoyant 'Silicon Glen'. A father of two, said: 'We're all just victims of an economic downturn here. It's just so shocking. What an awful Christmas.'

NEC senior manager said: 'People are just stunned and gutted. There's been lots of tears this morning. People are extremely sad about what's happened.'

The Livingston plant ceased production of D-RAM chips – which power personal computers – earlier this year and production of its advanced LSI chips will stop in March, leaving 1,260 people jobless.

In July, NEC made 600 people at the factory redundant in an effort to secure the future of the plant. However, a spokesman confirmed that due to a downturn in demand for mobile phone-related systems there was no sign of recovery.

Source: Frank O'Donnell, *The Scotsman*, 19 December 2001

Disney launches new Hong Kong theme park

● **Figure 1** Visitors having fun at Hong Kong Disneyland

Disney has opened a new US$1.8 billion (£1 billion) theme park in Hong Kong. Hong Kong Disneyland is expected to attract more than five-and-a-half million visitors in its first year.

The project is expected to generate US$19 billion over the next 40 years. Characters such as Alice in Wonderland sing and speak in Cantonese, while Chinese food is sold around the park.

Disney hopes the park will tap into Hong Kong's appeal to newly wealthy mainland Chinese and their children as a shopping and leisure centre.

When the project was first announced in 1999, it was expected that the park would create 6,000 jobs during construction, 18,000 jobs at the opening and 35,000 jobs over a 20-year period. A further 10,000 jobs were expected to be created by land reclamation projects and other associated works being funded by the government.

Source: the BBC News website, 12 September 2005

SUNSHINE HOLIDAYS ABROAD PUT BRITISH RESORTS IN SHADE

● **Figure 2** Neglected King's Street, Great Yarmouth

The decline of the British seaside holiday has had negative consequences for many coastal towns. Great Yarmouth, once a fashionable seaside town, was made accessible and popular by the arrival of the railway in 1844. However, since the 1970s, the package holiday abroad can now be afforded by more and more people – today, many people's holiday decisions take them to other countries. The result for Great Yarmouth was severe – employment fell by 23 per cent between 1991 and 2000. Parts of the town are among the most deprived areas in England.

Action Point

1. Make a table, or draw a diagram, to show the similarities between the three case studies above.
2. Write down what you think really caused the changes to the places in the Scottish and Hong Kong case studies.
3. If you can, visit a local travel agent. From the brochures on the shelves, try to decide which places are now fashionable and popular destinations for consumers. What might be the consequences for those places of their popularity?

Learning Point

Before we continue, let's check that you understand:
- the production-consumption chain
- how consumers' decisions can affect specific places
- the term 'interdependence'.

Chapter 6 Geographies of consumption

6.6 Who decides?

This section introduces a fieldwork exercise that you can do in your own home. The aim of the exercise is to investigate consumption decision-making in your household – who buys what, the reasons for their decision, and what might have influenced them, such as advertising, fashion, cost. When you have finished, you will have completed a short piece of research of your own.

Step 1
With a pen and notepad, explore your home. Make a list of around 10–15 items, such as electrical goods, clothing, food and furniture. Try to include some things that have been there for some time, and others that have been acquired more recently. Now, make a table like the one below, so that you can record your fieldwork.

Item and location	Who chose it (decision-maker)?	When and where was it acquired?	What influenced their decision?	Where was it made? (country of origin)

Step 2
Now the investigation work begins. By asking around at home, find out who made the decision to buy the item (it could be more than one person). Add this result to your table.

Step 3
The next research method you are going to use is an interview. You need to speak with each of the decision-makers you listed in step 2 above, and to ask them (a) about all the reasons they had in mind when they bought the particular item, and (b) whether they think they were influenced by cost, advertising, etc. (You could also find out whether they actually needed the item, or whether it was something they just wanted to have.)

Step 4
Write up your research in sections so that your aim, method, results and conclusions are clear to your readers. You can write in the past tense throughout. You could use the following headings:
Introduction and aims – set out what you were trying to discover, and why (perhaps include a map of the places you have found links to here).
Research methods – how did you undertake the investigation?
Results – present the completed table, and any other findings, together with a short description of what they seem to show.
Analysis – what do the results appear to mean? Can you answer the question you began with?
Conclusions and evaluation – did the investigation serve its purpose? Could it have been improved?

Well done – you have completed a short research project! You should now understand a little more about how complex the topic of consumption is.

Action Point
1. Plot the origins of the items you discovered on a world map, and use straight lines to join them with the place in which you live. How far have the items travelled? Do the decision-makers know that they have influenced people's lives in those places? Show them the map and see if they are surprised.
2. Compare the findings of your research with someone else who has completed the same exercise. Discuss your findings – are they similar or different?

6.7 The coolhunters

You may often use the word 'cool' to describe people or things. The idea of cool has an important part to play in the geography of consumption because products described in this way are almost guaranteed to be popular with many consumers.

The idea of cool is related to geography because it changes some people's behaviour. It also varies over space: cool is an idea mainly found in richer, **western countries**. It can be used to describe fashionable products that are in high demand. Cool products are bought in places (and by people) where incomes are sufficiently high for cool to succeed.

Cool is such a powerful concept that companies, particularly in the United States, employ '**coolhunters**' to carry out research with young people. Their job is to find out what people consider to be cool – their job is never-ending, because what is considered cool changes over time. The coolhunters' main task is to identify what the *next* cool thing is likely to be, so that the companies are ready to cash in. Cool is big business!

● **Figure 1** Cool in 2006, cool now?

The Rules of Cool

Rule 1: cool cannot be defined, only felt

Rule 2: cool can only be observed by those who are cool.

Rule 3: cool cannot be manufactured – *Jon Goss*

Source: www.thecoolhunter.net (2006)

Cool things are often consumed in huge quantities. We know that if something is consumed, it must be produced in the first place. It follows then that cool must be good for producers, and in turn the places where cool things are produced. Or does it? Cool status is temporary, so it is probably only temporary good news. When tastes change, and cool moves on, orders can fall and eventually cease.

Think Point

What might be the consequences for the people employed by producers of cool products? Does this mean there are consequences for particular places?

Think Point

Who benefits from cool?

Action Point

1. Write a job description for a coolhunter working in a company of your choice. Remember – a coolhunter is someone whose job it is to find out the next 'cool' product before it becomes cool.
2. Design an advertisement for product you consider to be cool. Is your design cool?
3. Is cool cool? Does it create losers as well as winners? Write a short, balanced report.

6.8 Fair trade

International trade is an important part of the world economy. It is responsible for billions of flows of money between countries every year. But some geographers are becoming concerned that international trade may put some often poorer, producer countries at a disadvantage. The purchasing and negotiating power of richer 'consumer' countries far outweighs that of less wealthy ones, and the prices producers are paid for products such as coffee and tea are relatively low – in some cases, they may not even cover the costs of production.

One way of increasing the **flows** of money from developed countries to **developing** ones is through Fairtrade products, a brand of 'ethical' products that aims to pay a fair price to producers of goods such as coffee, tea and sugar, and so improve the quality of life – including reducing poverty – in producer communities. Such products guarantee to give producers a price that covers their production costs and an additional amount that is invested in the local community.

> **Think Point**
> Why might richer countries have more negotiating power than poorer ones?

> **Think Point**
> The Fairtrade brand was launched in the Netherlands in the 1980s. Visit the Fairtrade website to find out about the organisation and a full list of products sold in British shops. Go to www.heinemann.co.uk/hotlinks, enter the express code 031XP and click on the link.

● **Figure 1** Picking Fairtrade tea

● **Figure 2** Sales of Fairtrade products in the UK in £ million, 1998–2004

	1998	1999	2000	2001	2002	2003	2004
Coffee	13.7	15.0	15.5	18.6	23.1	34.3	49.3
Tea	2.0	4.5	5.1	5.9	7.2	9.5	12.9
Chocolate/cocoa	1.0	2.3	3.6	6.0	7.0	10.9	16.5
Honey products	n/a	>0.1	0.9	3.2	4.9	6.1	3.4
Bananas	n/a	n/a	7.8	14.6	17.3	24.3	30.6
Other	n/a	n/a	n/a	2.2	3.5	7.2	27.3
TOTAL	16.7	21.8	32.9	50.5	63.0	92.3	140.0

Source: the Fairtrade website

● Figure 3 Where Fairtrade products are produced

Cocoa	Coffee	Fresh fruit and juice	Flowers	Honey	Sugar	Tea	Wines
Belize Bolivia Dominican Republic Ghana	Cameroon Colombia Costa Rica Dom. Republic East Timor Ethiopia Guatemala Haiti Honduras Indonesia Mexico Nicaragua Peru Rwanda Sumatra Tanzania Uganda Papua New Guinea	Brazil Burkino Faso Costa Rica Cuba Dominican Republic Ecuador Egypt Ghana Windward Islands	Kenya	Chile Mexico Uruguay	Malawi Paraguay	India Kenya Sri Lanka Tanzania Uganda	Chile South Africa

Source: the Fairtrade website

Think Point

Why do you think consumers buy Fairtrade products? Is it just to help people in poorer countries?

In 2006, there were more than 1,500 Fairtrade products available in UK shops, ranging from orange juice to chocolate, and from bananas to tea.

Some facts about Fairtrade

- Countries selling Fairtrade products: 20
- Countries producing Fairtrade products: 51 – in Africa, Asia and Latin America
- UK sales of Fairtrade products (2004): £140 million
- Fairtrade producer organisations: 548
- Number of families involved in FairTrade production: 800,000 (equivalent to about 5 million people)

Source: the Fairtrade website

There are other products that are fairly traded, but which do not carry the well-known Fairtrade brand. Examples come from Oxfam and Traidcraft, among others; the Co-op supermarket has established its own fair trade brand.

Action Point

1. Look at the table showing sales of Fairtrade products in the UK. Produce a graph to show the increase in sales by product. Consider, which type of graph would be appropriate. Remember that presentation and accuracy are vital in graphs.
2. Look at the table showing the countries where Fairtrade products are produced. Produce a map that shows clearly the origins of the different Fairtrade products. What patterns can you identify in the map?
3. If you have access to the Internet, use the Fairtrade website to identify the countries in which Fairtrade products are sold to consumers. Mark them clearly on the map you produced above. What patterns can you now identify in the map as a whole?

Assessment

It is often said that the best geographers do not stop when they understand some of the problems of the world, but they take action to make a difference.

Put yourself in the position of a geographer who wants to 'make a difference'. Design a campaign for your school that aims to persuade pupils, staff and parents of the benefits of fairly traded products. You may wish to use websites to help you to gather information about fair trade campaigns, but this is not essential if you do not have Internet access.

Your work should include the following:
- Describe the campaign, and how you would put it into practice.
- Explain the way in which you designed the campaign.
- Include an overview of the key points that your campaign needs to address.
- Predict how successful your campaign would be in influencing pupils, staff and parents – how much of a difference could you make?

Take care to use an appropriate form of writing, remembering the need for accurate spelling and grammar.

Glossary

Activity space – the network of all the places people visit

Bottom-up planning – where local people influence the planning process
Built environment – the combination of buildings and spaces in a settlement

Climate – average of the weather conditions over a long period of time
Climate change – the warming or cooling of the earth's atmosphere
Clone town – a place which seems to have lost its local uniqueness
Cocacolonisation – spread of western or American values
Consumption – the products or experiences that people buy
Consumption landscape – the effects of consumption on the physical landscape, e.g. shopping centres
Coolhunter – someone who searches for the next cool products
Cybergeography – the geography of cyberspace
Cybermap – a map of cyberspace
Cyberspace – an invisible place formed by the joining together of ICTS, such as telephones, the Internet or satellite television

Dendrochonology – study of growth rings in tree trunks
Digital divide – the differences between those who are connected to the Internet and those who are not

Extreme weather events – unusual or "freak" weather, such as intense storms

Flow – a movement of people, goods, service and money between places

Garden city – Ebenezer Howard's idea to build new settlements in the countryside
Geography of consumption – the study of people's expenditure over space
Geography of exclusion – the study of places from which people are denied access in some way, by a physical or human barrier
Global brand – a company's name or logo which is well-known in many countries worldwide, such as IBM
Global company – a company trading worldwide
Global warming – the warming up of the earth's atmosphere (*climate change* is a more neutral term)
Globalisation – the changes that places and people around the globe are experiencing because the world is becoming better connected
Green belt – the land around some towns and cities where building is not permitted

Information superhighway – large, fast and electronic flows of information, such as the Internet
Infrastructure – a large physical network, such as a road or communications system
Interdependence – the idea that places rely on each other, usually in the buying and selling of goods and services

Local Development Framework – a local authority's plan for the development of an area

New Towns – planned towns built on greenfield sites to accommodate people and businesses moving out of older cities

Out-of-town shopping centre – a purpose-built shopping area containing large retail outlets in a non-central location

Physical matter – solid particles

Place – the locations we know ourselves, which mean something to us or those with which we have a connection (as opposed to *space*)

Precipitation – water falling to earth in a variety of forms, e.g. rain, snow, hail

Production-consumption chain – the connections between a product being made or grown and its end-user

Quality of life – a measure of how well-off people are, not just in terms of money but also emotionally

Regeneration – the renewal of run-down or deprived places

Regional shopping centre – a very large purpose-built shopping mall in non-central location

Ria – a flooded valley

Sense of place – the distinctive characteristics or features that make a place unique

Shrinking world – places seeming to become closer together, caused by the speeding up of long-distance travel and communications

Space – places with which we have no connection, or no feeling towards (as opposed to *place*)

Suburb – the outer parts of towns and cities, usually combining large residential areas with local shopping and employment

Sustainability – using the earth's resources at such a rate that we leave behind enough for generations to come

Top-down planning – where the government controls the planning process, and imposes changes on local people

Topophilia – a love of (a particular) place; the bond between people and places

Topophobia – a fear of (a particular) place

Settlement – a place where people live, such as a hamlet, village, town, city or conurbation

Weather – the current state of the atmosphere

Index

Page number in *italics* refer to diagrams and illustrations

Aberdeen *10*
air travel, developements 53, *53*

Birmingham 6
   attitudes to 6–7
   local planning in 44–5, *44*
Booth, Charles 35
brands, globalisation 58–9, *58*

changes over space, places 10, *10*
changes over time, places 10, *10*
climate
   see also climate change
   definitions 16–17
   England *16*
   landscape influences *17*
climate change 17
   debate for and against 28
   evidence
      dendrochronology 20, *20*
      geological patterns 21
      historical records 21, *21*
      ice core analysis 20
      landscapes 20, *20*
      pollen analysis 20
      sediment core analysis 20
   global warming 19, *19*
   human causes, enhanced greenhouse gases 24–5
   international debate 29
   national initiatives 30, *31*
   natural causes
      dust clouds 23
      greenhouse effect 23, *23*
      interstellar material 22
      irregular orbit 22
      sunspots 22
   past 140 years 18–19, *19*
   past 850m years 18, *18*
   personal initiatives 31
   and planning process 40–1
   temperatures, predicted rises 26–7, *26*
Coca-Cola 64–5, *64*
Coin Street Community (London) 46–7, *46*, *47*

communications
   see also information and communications technology
   electronics 54–5
consumers 88
   demands of 89
   rights 89
consumption 88
   and decision-making 89, 94, *94*, 95, 96
   environmental impact 90
cool products 97
corner shops 92, *92*
countries
   developing 62, 65
   global power 60
Crieff (Perthshire) *10*
cybercafes 70, *70*
cyberspace
   definitions 68, *68*
   flows within 73, *73*
   holes in 82–3
   images of *80*
   Interoute network *81*
   maps of 78, *78*
   mobile teleworking 75, *75*

decision-making
   and consumption 89, 94, *94*, 95
   process of 96
dendrochronology, and climate change 20, *20*
developing countries
   global companies 62, 64–5, *65*
   money flows to 98
disabled people
   enabled by ICT 75
   exclusion of 12
dust clouds, climate changes due to 23

Earth
   irregular orbit 22
   solar radiation on 22, *22*
emails 71
England, climate *16*
enhanced greenhouse effect 24–5
environment
   see also planned environment; planning processes

Index 103

new towns 37–9, *38*, *39*
Nike 62–3, *62*, *63*
nitrous oxide 24
North Atlantic Drift, possible changes to 27

oceans, North Atlantic Drift 27
online shopping
   future of 84–5
   growth of 84
out-of-town shopping centres 91, *91*

philanthropists 35
place
   'my' 4–5, *4*
   representations of 3, *3*, 8
   a sense of 3, *3*, 8
places
   attitudes to 6–7
   changes over space 10, *10*
   changes over time 10, *10*
   definitions 2
   distinctive features 3, *3*
   emotional reactions to 13, *13*
   excluded 12, *12*, 13
   holiday representations 9, *9*
   interdependence 9, *9*
   urban *2*
planned environment 34
   garden cities 36–7, *36*, *37*
   new towns 37–9, *38*
planning processes 40–1, *40*
   at local levels 46–7, *46*, *47*
   at regional levels 42–3, *42*, *43*
plants, climate changes and 26
pollen analysis, and climate change 20
poverty, London 35
production-consumption chains 93, *93*

rainfall patterns, predicted changes 26
regeneration, urban 43, 44–5
regional planning processes 42–3, *42*, *43*
regional shopping centres 90, *90*
representations of place 11, *11*
rights, consumers 89
rivers, rates of discharges 26

sediment core analysis, and climate change 20
sense of place 3, *3*
   uniqueness 8, *8*
shopping, online 84–5

shopping centres
   out-of-town 91, *91*
   regional 90, *91*
shops, corner 92, *92*
Singapore 76, *76*
   National Information Infrastructure 76–7
spaces, activity 2, *2*
Staffa *11*
suburbs 4
sunspots, climate changes due to 22
sustainability 36, 44

telephone networks
   global 72
   mobile connections 78
teleworking 75, *75*
temperatures, predicted rises 25, *25*
topophilia 13, *13*
topophobia 13, *13*
towns, 'cloning' of 59
trade, international fair 98–9
travel, speeding up of 52–3, *52*

U-shaped glacial valleys 20, *20*
UK Climates Impact Programme (UKCIP) 30, *31*
urban places 2
urban regeneration 43, 44–5
US dominance, ICT 74

Victorian London 35, *35*
virtual reality 72, *72*

weather
   definitions 16
   increase in extreme 27
world wide web 71
   development 34
environmental impact, consumption 90
excluded places 12, *12*, 13

fair trade 98–9
flows 56–7, *56*, *57*
   of goods 88, 93
   information 70
   within cyberspace 73, *73*
fossil fuels 24

garden cities 36–7, *36*, *37*
geological patterns, and climate change 21
glacial melting 26

glacial valleys 20, *20*
global companies
   definitions 62
   developing countries 62
global power
   countries 60
   multi-national companies 60–3, *61, 62, 63*
global products 64–5, *64*
global telephone networks 72
global warming 19, *19*
   see also climate change
globalisation
   brands 58–9, *58*
   definitions 51
   examples 50–1
   flows 56–7, *56, 57*
goods
   flows of 88, 93
   production-consumption chains 93, *93*
greenhouse effect
   climate changes due to 23, *23*
   enhanced 24–5
greenhouse gases 23

halocarbons 25
historical records, and climate change 21, *21*
holidays
   decision-making 94–5, *94, 95*
   representation of places 11
Howard, Sir Ebenezer 36–7

ice core analysis, and climate change 20
information, flows of 70
information and communications technology
   (ICT) 68–9
   effects of 74–5
   emails 71
   global telephone networks 72
   Internet 70
   Internet chatrooms 71
   networks 68, *69*
   Singapore 76–7
   US dominance 74
   virtual reality 72, *72*
   world wide web 71

interdependence
   places 9, *9*, 36
   production-consumption chains 93, *93*
international fair trade 98–9
Internet 70
   access to 82–3, *82, 83*
   chatrooms 71
   exclusion from 83, *83*
   traffic 1993 78, *78*
Interoute network *81*
interstellar material, climate changes due to 22
irregular orbit, climate changes due to 22
IT2000, Singapore 76–7

Kyoto Protocol 1997 29

landscapes
   and climate change 20, *20*
   climate influences *17*
London 3, 8, *8*
   Coin Street Community 46–7, *46, 47*
   poverty 35
   Victorian 35, *35*

methane 24
Milton Keynes 38–9, *38, 39*
mobile telephone connections 78
mobile teleworking 75, *75*
Mull, Isle of 11
multi-national companies, global power 60–3,
   61, 62, 63
'my place' 4, *4*
   presenting 4–5

National Information Infrastructure IT2000,
   Singapore 76–7